Joseph Shield Nicholson

Thoth

A Romance

Joseph Shield Nicholson

Thoth
A Romance

ISBN/EAN: 9783744775472

Printed in Europe, USA, Canada, Australia, Japan

Cover: Foto ©Thomas Meinert / pixelio.de

More available books at **www.hansebooks.com**

THOTH

A ROMANCE

THIRD EDITION

WILLIAM BLACKWOOD AND SONS
EDINBURGH AND LONDON
MDCCCLXXXIX

PREFACE TO THE SECOND EDITION.

I GLADLY avail myself of this occasion to thank my critics for the very friendly reception they have accorded to a book which was issued, in the fullest meaning of the term, anonymously —that is to say, even without the knowledge of a single personal friend. At the same time, I wish to make an explanation which is partly of the nature of a protest.

Post hoc ergo propter hoc may not always be a fallacy, but it was certainly a mistake on the part of several reviewers of 'Thoth' to translate it in their haste, "after 'She,' therefore on account of 'She.'" For, as a matter of fact, 'Thoth' was designed and in part composed more than twelve years ago. In its present form, however, it has been entirely rewritten. It may interest some

of my critics to know the original intention and
scheme, and the reasons why I delayed the pub-
lication even longer than the classical ninth year.

The original idea was philosophical. I wished
to illustrate the power of will and intellect
working through generations with a definite
design, and to show that this power might be
used for the most repulsive object. The object
I chose for my purpose was the destruction of
the whole human race by means of pestilences,
with the intention of replacing it with a race of
men who had for generations been trained in the
exercise of the highest intelligence. The new
rule was to be a tyranny of intellect. The original designer of this scheme was supposed to be
an Egyptian, who had discovered a method of
suspending animation. His attempt to introduce
the government of intellect amongst existing
races had failed, and he determined to destroy
them, even if it took thousands of years to prepare the means. The defeat of the scheme in the
original plan was due to the friendship of the
latest Thoth for Philetos. Philetos was, in marked
contrast to these haters of men, a man whom
every one loved, and who was the *beau idéal* of
a philanthropist. Thus the victory over hate
in the original plan was gained by friendship.

The reigning Thoth introduced the plague at Athens, and his life was saved by Philetos. Afterwards Thoth attempted on three occasions to kill his friend, fearing the power of his friendship. The climax was reached in a scene in which the ancestral Thoth and his descendants were aroused, and the fate of the world was to depend on the decision of the ancient ruler.

After writing a considerable part of 'Thoth' on this plan, I became dissatisfied for several reasons. In the first place, friendship alone, though in the ancient world one of the strongest passions, did not seem as I worked it out strong enough for my purpose. I had introduced also, in the last scene, a supernatural element of a purely imaginary kind, and I heartily disliked the *deus ex machinâ* even when of my own making. I also considered the style inflated and the characters far too abstract. The original idea, however, seemed worth developing; and when I took it up again after an interval of ten years, I substituted Daphne and love for Philetos and friendship, and put more of the elements of common humanity into the characters. I discarded the supernatural altogether, for however wonderful Thoth's powers are, there is nothing beyond the possibility of modern science. Even the destruction of the city in the end is due to the want of a guiding mind.

I have perhaps said enough to clear myself from the charge, never very hardly pressed, of conscious or unconscious imitation; but as it may interest some of my readers, I print in an appendix the last chapter as it originally stood.

THE AUTHOR.

CONTENTS.

THOTH.

PROLOGUE.

BY THE CELEBRATED PHILOSOPHER AND PHYSICIAN XENOPHILOS.

NOTHING is more difficult than to separate the true from the false in a narrative in which it is necessary for the most part to rely on the testimony of one person only, and that person a woman whose mind had been shaken by extraordinary perils and vicissitudes. A task so laborious I shall not attempt, but shall simply set forth in order what Daphne, the daughter of Phi-

A

letos, told me in fragments at various times, although I confess that some things seem in their nature impossible.

This much, however, I will say for the benefit of posterity, and that it may not be imagined this writing is from beginning to end the figment of a poet's fancy: Daphne was, without question, by far the most beautiful woman of her time, and excited a most violent and extreme passion in some of the wisest and most celebrated Athenians, before the events occurred which I am about to record. And I do not think it at all incredible that a man, driven by the madness of his love for her, should be induced to sacrifice everything he held most dear. Nor do I think it wonderful, considering the haughty ambition of many of no great worth or power, that a man who had a marvellous genius in making discoveries of the hidden nature of things, should try to emulate the might of far - darting Apollo, who in his anger slays people in multitudes by the shafts of his plagues and pestilences. And if any one should think the conduct of this Egyptian and his ancestors, as manifested in their deeds, altogether contrary to human nature (as if one should say that doves chased hawks, or any other creature acted in a way quite different from its kind), I would not only remind him of the horrible and perverse sins even of Greeks in former times, but would also ask him to remember that for ages the Egyptians had been soured by a gloomy and cruel superstition.

Then, again, as to all the matters which are said to have occurred in Athens, I have made the most careful inquiries, and, even in the most minute particulars, I find that the testimony of Daphne is confirmed.

But to him who will be admonished, this

narrative, whether true or false, certainly declares that no human skill or strength of purpose can altogether conquer nature and chance, and may thus serve, like the tragedies of our poets, as a notable warning against pride and presumption.

CHAPTER I.

THE PLAGUE AND THE MERCHANTS.

In the time of Pericles, as every one knows, Athens attained her greatest glory. Magnificent buildings were erected, and in them were placed statues and other ornaments of most exquisite workmanship. Whilst the work was in progress, great encouragement was given to foreign merchants, who brought materials of various kinds, and especially ivory and metals. The laws against strangers were in a great measure relaxed, and they were enabled to prosecute their business with as much freedom as the citizens themselves. Even after the outbreak of the Peloponnesian war, and when fear of spies and treachery was natural, there was still a great concourse of foreign merchants in the port and the city.

But an event occurred which soon put to flight all strangers, and made Athens an object of the utmost dread. This was the great plague, of which Thucydides, the son of Oloros, has given a memorable account in his history.

A most remarkable incident, however, which is the key-stone of this narrative, he has omitted to notice, probably because, being incredible in its nature, he ascribed it to the invention of those whose minds had been affected by the horrors of the scene, and considered it to be unworthy of the dignity of his style and his careful adherence to truth.

A few days before the outbreak of the

plague, a company of merchants, about a
score in number, arrived at Athens. They
gave out that their native land was Egypt,
but they had been trading with many
Grecian cities at peace with Athens. They
seemed to be extremely wealthy, and their
merchandise consisted mainly of ivory and
gems. They had also abundance of gold
and silver. They acted as if they did not
speak or understand the Greek tongue, and
always transacted their affairs by means
of interpreters. They appeared to be very
careless or ignorant in their bargains, often
selling their wares for a much less price
than, with a little trouble and inquiry, they
might have obtained.

They made no purchases themselves,
with one exception, and in this particular
they were most fastidious and difficult to
please. They showed the greatest anxiety
to buy young female slaves, and they exer-

cised the greatest care in the selection.
They not only demanded beauty and health,
but inquired carefully into their education
and abilities.   It was generally complained
that it was impossible to satisfy the de-
mands of the merchants, as they appeared
to apply tests which neither the women nor
their owners could understand.

As soon as the plague appeared, which
happened first of all in the port, all
foreigners, with the exception of these
Egyptians, fled away in their ships.   They,
however, in spite of the dissatisfaction
they expressed with the slaves offered for
sale, not only lingered on, but appeared
to be quite regardless of the dangers of
infection.

Yet, in truth, both the disease and the circumstances of the plague-stricken city were
such as to shake the courage of the bravest.

For, as the historian narrates, suddenly, without any apparent cause preceding, people who seemed in perfect health were seized with an extreme ache in their heads, and redness and inflammation of the eyes; then inwardly their throats and tongues grew presently bloody, and their breath became noisome and unsavoury. Thereupon followed sneezing and hoarseness, and, not long after, the pain, together with a mighty cough, came down into the breast. As the disease spread, most dreadful weakness and, in most cases, strong convulsions ensued. The bodies of the afflicted outwardly to the touch were not very hot, but inwardly they so burned as not to endure the lightest clothes or linen garment, and they would fain have cast themselves into the cold water. Their thirst was insatiable, and those who were not looked after ran to the wells; but whether they drank much or

little, they got neither ease nor power of
sleep. Many suffered for seven or nine
days, and then died of the inner burning,
while yet their strength seemed undi-
minished; others survived the torment,
and then died of weakness. Some escaped
with the loss of their eyes or the extremi-
ties of the limbs, and others were so much
stricken in mind that they remembered
neither themselves nor their acquaintances.
And the sickness, and the cruelty wherewith it handled each one, far surmounted
all expression in words—it was so griev-
ous and terrible.

But the greatest misery of all was the
dejection of mind in such as found themselves beginning to be sick, for they grew
presently desperate, and gave themselves
over without making any resistance. Many
died like sheep affected by mutual visita-
tion; and some, forsaken and forlorn, for

want of such as should take care of
them.

The mortality was greatly increased by
the crowds of country people who, on
account of the war, had come into the city
with their goods and chattels, and having
no homes, they lived in stifling booths and
in tents. Dying men lay tumbling one
upon another in the streets, and about
every spring and conduit. The temples,
also, were full of dead, for, oppressed with
the violence of the calamity, and not knowing what to do, men grew careless even of
holy things. The laws which they former-
ly used touching funerals were all broken.
When one had made a funeral pile, another
getting before him would throw in his dead
and give it fire. And when one was burning, another would come, and having cast
therein him whom he carried, go his way
again. Yet up to that time no feeling

amongst the Athenians was more profound
than their respect for the dead.

The city was filled with wailing, horror,
and loathsomeness, but in the midst of
despair there were frantic outbursts of out-
rageous pleasures. Licentiousness was un-
bridled, and men grasped at wild delights
as if they held their lives but by the day.
The rich died, and the poor, who had never
dreamed of riches, slipped into their places,
and, thinking they had not a moment to
lose, made their only aim the speedy fru-
ition of their goods. Neither the fear of
the gods nor the laws of men awed any
man. For it seemed all one, to worship
or not to worship, seeing that all alike
perished, and no one expected his life
would last till he received punishment of
his crimes by human judgment. Many
thought that the whole city would be destroyed, and hastened to enjoy some little

part of their lives. Women left their apartments, and, without friends or guardians, rushed to the temples or tried to flee from the pestilence beyond the city bounds. For all discipline was broken through, and all did what seemed good to them.

In spite of these dreadful scenes, the Egyptians showed no signs of haste or alarm, and seemed to regard the terror-stricken people with mingled curiosity and contempt. At first this conduct was ascribed to the gloomy nature of their religion, and to the fact that in their own cities the plague was said to be never altogether stilled. But gradually a rumour spread that they had in their possession some drug or charm by which they made themselves proof against the pestilence.

In a short time they were surrounded by a tumultuous throng of men and women.

A deafening outcry arose of threats and
entreaties. Some tried to embrace the
knees of the merchants, and offered them
masses of gold and precious stones ; others
shrieked like madmen, " Give us life,—save
us ! " Some, on the other hand, tried to
terrify them with brandished weapons ;
whilst others, hoping more from prayers,
threatened the threateners, and assumed
the part of defenders of the strangers, ap-
pealing to Zeus, the god of hospitality.

As the tumult grew, and the pressure of
the crowd increased, the merchants, speaking in an unknown tongue, seemed to ad-
dress one who appeared to be their leader,
in terms of remonstrance and expostula-
tion, mingled, however, with respect and
submission. No interpreter could be found,
so that no one could understand what was
said except vaguely from the looks and
gestures of the speakers.

Suddenly, the leader made signs as if asking for silence and attention, and a thrill of astonishment passed through the crowd as he began to speak in a language which many of the people could, with a little difficulty, understand. It seemed an ancient dialect of Greek, in most respects like that used by Homer in his poems.

"Men of Athens," he said, "ye wonder that we seem unmoved in the midst of this dreadful plague, and ye think that we have some charm or drug wherewith we defend ourselves from the infection. But we indeed are careless, because death by the pestilence seems to us no worse than the doom with which we are threatened if we escape. We come from a country beyond Egypt, and are the descendants of a remnant of Greeks who for many generations have been held in honourable captivity by the powerful princes of the land. We have preserved our own customs, and as ye see, our own language, and we have served as priests to our masters. And often the daughters of our race have been chosen as queens, and till a little time ago everything went well with us. Then certain Greeks appeared, who aroused the envy of our king and his princes by telling of the glories of Athens, and praising, most of all, the beauty and the wit of the Athenian women, and they have sent us, not only to bring back a faithful report of the grandeur of your city, but they have ordered us to bring a number of your most beautiful and best educated maidens, to become wives of the king and his nobles. In the meantime they hold those Greeks in captivity, and also our wives and children, and they have threatened us and them with dreadful punishment if we do not bring back the maidens; and we thought at first to purchase slaves, but we fear detection, for how can slaves make fitting queens? But now the plague which has struck down your people seems to offer us some hope of safety. For, perhaps, some of your maidens, being without protectors in this calamity, will themselves be willing to go with us, or their guardians, fearing the worst, will send them. And in token of our good faith, we have brought large stores of precious things to leave with you, and we will bind ourselves with great oaths that the maidens shall be dealt with in the most honourable manner. And as regards this pestilence, we can indeed offer you no certain cure, but we would earnestly warn you, knowing something of the matter by sad experience, that your only hope of safety is in avoiding crowds, and keeping as much apart as possible. But see for yourselves the truth of my words."

And as he spoke thus, several persons in the throng were suddenly taken with the plague, and terror seized on the rest, and they broke up and fled. Many of the maidens, however, remained, believing through the extremity of their fear that it was best for them to go with the Egyptians.

And although it would be easy for any one sitting quietly at home in the enjoyment of calm prosperity to consider the tale which they told as unworthy of credence, it was a very different matter under the actual circumstances of the case. And, as will appear in the sequel, there was as much truth as falsehood in the promises, and the falsehood was chiefly of that kind which consists in the suppression of truth. One thing at least was certain, and was calculated to impress the senses. They had undoubtedly a large amount of treasure, of which they seemed quite careless. Besides this, it was known that they had made endeavours to purchase female slaves for their purpose. But, above everything else, the minds even of men of courage and philosophers had been shaken in the terror, and it was natural for young maidens to believe in anything which seemed to promise them a chance of safety from a horrible death.

In a short time more than thirty of the fairest young women of Athens had promised to go on board the Egyptian vessel; and to these, that no doubt might shake them at the last, the leader told a thing still more wonderful. He said, with an appearance of the greatest secrecy, that they had a charm by which a small number could be protected against the plague, and that they had failed to mention this because its virtue would cease if applied beyond this small number. Then he painted, in the most glowing language, the delights and pleasures which would be their lot in the distant land. He also proceeded to terrify those whom he was unwilling to take, and the maidens he had chosen began to fear now that others might take their place, and promised to do all he bade them.

CHAPTER II.

DAPHNE.

YET, in spite of the promises which the Egyptian made, and the unspeakable terror of the maidens on account of the plague, it is doubtful if they would have consented to go at the last had it not been for Daphne.

For when the men had fled and most of the maidens, and only those remained whom the stranger had chosen, and to whom he was telling flattering tales in order to take away their dread, Daphne suddenly appeared, having heard of what had taken place.

It chanced that all her family had been taken by the plague, and she was left quite alone,—for, as was well known, she was a native of Miletus. She had been brought by her parents to Athens as a young girl, owing to some political troubles, and was at this time less than twenty years old; and to make this narrative clear to those of a later time who may chance to read it, something must be said of the character of Daphne before these adventures began.

First of all, she was strong of will, and rather ruled than obeyed her parents; and she not only obstinately refused an honourable marriage, but spoke bitterly of the small esteem and respect in which the Athenians held their lawful wives; and she upheld as a model Aspasia, her compatriot, the friend of Pericles, and in all but name his honoured wife. For, whilst

the lawful wives of the noblest Athenians
were cooped up like children in their own
apartments, Aspasia enjoyed perfect freedom, and was entertained of the brightest
wits and the wisest and bravest of Athens;
and she was knit to Pericles with ties of
most ardent affection, far stronger than
any bonds fastened by a forced contract,
and she was honoured and treated as were
the consorts of noble Greeks in olden times,
and not regarded merely as a nurse for her
husband's children.

And Daphne had determined, in like
manner, to enter into no forced marriage,
but to form a fitting connection with some
man whom she loved and honoured, if
chance so willed it, in marriage, but if not,
even as Aspasia with Pericles. And what
may perhaps to some seem strange, whilst
she had constantly asserted for herself the
truest freedom, she had preserved also the

strictest virtue.   Many Athenian youths
had loved her, and some men of good
standing, but none had touched her fancy.
Like Aspasia, she had been carefully
trained in poetry, rhetoric, and music,
and she could converse with much acute-
ness and in a pleasing manner.

Now, when the plague had carried off
her natural protectors and desolated the
city, Daphne not only despaired in her
heart of carrying out her idea in practice,
but was afraid for her life, and at the least
dreaded that her beauty would be marred
or the sharpness of her mind blunted.

And when she was thus cast down in
spirit, a maiden of her acquaintance came
running, and told her all the Egyptian had
promised, saying that they were themselves
of Grecian stock, and spoke the language
of the old heroes.

And Daphne, although she thought the

report an idle tale or a snare, still, seeing
that it offered some chance of safety, whilst
in the city there seemed none, agreed to
hear what the stranger had to say.

She found the maidens in a group
apart, weeping and terrified, and taking
counsel together; but the Egyptians were
talking to one another in an unknown
tongue, and laughing, as it were, over a
good jest. To Daphne, however, there
seemed to be more bitterness than mirth
in their laughter, and she swiftly determined not to go, and to dissuade the
others also. But suddenly the leader
turned his eyes full upon her, and she felt
compelled, as if by some superior power,
to scan his features closely, and to try
to pierce his thoughts.

He was of ordinary stature, and evidently in the full vigour of manhood.
His frame was strong, and his appearance

denoted the perfection of health ; but he did not appear to be trained in athletic exercises in the Greek manner, and his whole bearing was that of a man accustomed to work more with the mind than the body. His forehead was, both in height and breadth, much more massive than was customary with the Athenians. His hair, which was cut very short, and his eyebrows, were perfectly black. He wore no beard, and the fineness of his skin, although darker than that of even Asiatics, seemed almost boyish. His nose and mouth were of the pure Greek type, and the setting of his lips and chin denoted great determination. His eyes, however, formed by far the most striking feature of his person. They were deeply seated under overhanging brows, but their large fulness and intense blackness made them at once seize the attention of the beholder. Even in

momentary repose they displayed a wonderful and mysterious depth of intelligence, but the rapid restless motion with
which they generally absorbed every detail
in the range of sight, revealed a marvellous
power of observation and quickness of
decision. Their glances seemed to pene-
trate the inmost recesses of the mind; and
the Greek maiden knew at once that she
had never seen such power in any countenance, and she felt at first sight the influence of a mighty will.

Daphne was in most respects in striking
contrast to the Egyptian leader.

She was more than his equal in the
exquisite proportions of her limbs, and
she was in the very spring-time of youthful beauty. But her forehead, though
broad, was low, and showed no trace of the
oppression of thought. Her eyes were like
those of the goddesses in Homer, whom,

confident in the truth of nature, he boldly praised as being ox-eyed. They seemed as if formed for the display of all the tenderness and longing of the highest human love, but sensuous and passionate they were not, and everything in Daphne's appearance betokened a well-balanced and restful mind.

Woman she was in perfection, of the purest Greek race, with the soft outlines of a beauty moulded by feeling, with lips ready to respond to affection or to reject scorn with passionate impulse, with a hand soft for caresses, or when knit with anger, strong as the Amazon's in battle. Power her face showed in abundance, but it was the power of the varying instinct that has reason for its instrument, and utterly unlike that of the Egyptian, in which a glance seemed to show that every passion was under the control of an iron

will, and guided by reason only. The
woman moved with easy grace, as if every
gesture was a pleasure, whilst every
movement of the man betokened restless,
untiring energy.

When the Egyptian leader saw Daphne
with the maidens who had already agreed
to make the venture, he first of all seemed
astonished at her radiant beauty and her
composure of manner, and then said :—

"We had completed the number of those
whom we would take, but come thou too if
thou wilt, for thou art a goddess-queen
amongst the others."

But she answered—"It seems as if ye
wished to take advantage of our terror and
steal us away for slaves, for your tale is
difficult to believe. Ye boast yourselves to
be Greeks, but many tribes of Grecians have
I seen, and none with features and hair like

yours; and ye speak not Greek to one another, and the language thou thyself speakest seems learned from the books of old
poets, and not thy mother's tongue."

Then the leader replied—"These men
are my servants, and through dwelling
long among strangers our appearance has
changed."

And Daphne had from the first been constrained to admit that his countenance
seemed much more noble and kingly than
the rest; but she said, " Give me some sign
that these are thy servants. Why does
that man," pointing to one of them, " sneer
at me and laugh so immoderately?"

Then the leader said, " Here is a sign for
thee."

And going up to the man, he struck him
full in the face, and the blood started from
his lips, and the man fell as one dead, yet
none of his companions said a word.

Then Daphne believed in his authority, but she was alarmed by his violence and turned to go. But he said to her—

"Wilt thou indeed go back to a loathsome death when life and honour and riches are open to thee? Wouldst thou through silly fear become like him?" and he pointed to a man at a little distance writhing in the agony of the plague. "I can save thee if thou wilt. See, the plague has no terror for me."

Then he went up to the sick man and took him by the hand, and looked steadfastly in his face and said, "Thou art fortunate—thou wilt not die of this disease."

And another plague-stricken wretch near him begged with parched lips for water, but he said, "Too late!" and turned to Daphne.

"Take care it is not too late for thee! We have already more than enough who are willing to go. Still it vexes me to leave the loveliest to black death, and to save others. What more dost thou desire to know or to make me promise?" and he seemed to speak and look in a more kindly manner than before. And suddenly through Daphne's mind there flashed the words of the poet, "Rather would I live on earth as the hireling of another with a landless man who had no great livelihood, than bear sway among all the dead that be departed." Then she said, "Promise me one thing. Swear to me by thy strongest oath, and I will go. Swear to me if, when I reach thy country, I like it not, thou wilt send me back unharmed either to Athens or to some Greek city which has escaped the pestilence."

And he said, "By the respect I owe to my fathers, who are not dead but sleep, awaiting the day of triumph, I swear to thee. It is an oath that cannot be broken."

And his dark eyes flashed, and no sign of deceit appeared in his face; and Daphne said, "I trust thee. I will go."

And the other maidens gained confidence by what they had seen and heard, and, according to the word of the Egyptian leader, went by different ways and as secretly as possible to a place appointed for meeting, and they said nothing to any they met.

CHAPTER III.

NEPENTHE.

BEFORE they separated, the Egyptian leader gave to Daphne, whom he looked on as having authority over the rest, a powdered substance in a small linen bag.

"This," said he, "is that Nepenthe of which your poet sings, the most soothing of all medicines, and known to the Egyptians from very ancient times. When ye come to our trysting-place on the coast, and the other maidens begin to be again afraid, mix this drug with sweet wine and they will forget their sorrow. Say to them that it is a remedy against the plague. As

soon as ye have partaken of it, we will
appear and take you to our ship. And in
the ship ye shall find the female slaves we
have brought, and good store of garments
and precious things. So care for nothing
but to escape as speedily as possible, for if
the reason of your flight were known, all
the Athenians would come, and in the
crowd all must perish. Farewell!"

The place of meeting was a little sandy
bay set in the midst of steep, rough rocks,
and about two hours from the city. Encouraged by the spirit and example of Daphne
on the one hand, and on the other driven
by the fear of the plague, the maidens, a
little before sunset, reached the appointed
spot. At some distance they saw a dark
vessel unlike any they had ever seen, for
there seemed to be place neither for oars
nor sails. It looked rather like the hull of

a wrecked ship than a vessel prepared for
a long journey.

The maidens in their trepidation were
ready to start with alarm at any strange
sight, and the black vessel, on which not
a man was visible, seemed to them as
dismal as the boat with which Charon
ferries the souls of the dead over the Styx.
They looked back already with longing to
the city, and with fear they saw the long
shadows cast by the declining sun.

But Daphne was determined to complete
the venture, and she prepared to give them
the drug.

"This," said she, "is a charm against the
plague."

"Perchance," whispered one of the
maidens, "it is poisonous."

But Daphne replied, "Nay, that thought
of thine is altogether foolish. Why should
the men entice us away from the city

simply to put us to death? Fear not,—I will begin."

She mixed the nepenthe with the sweet wine, and drank of it herself, and gave to the others, and they all drank.

And then, indeed, as the leader of the band of merchants had said, so it happened.

Slowly and dreamily the distant city began to blend with the clouds. The waves of the sea fell upon the shore with the rhythm of sweet music. The air became heavy with the odours of drowsy flowers and mystic perfumes. The sand formed a softer couch than the most exquisite cushions of the East. The maidens looked on one another with calm content. Fearless and careless, they gave themselves up to the misty shapes of languid pleasures.

All memory of the past vanished, and vanished also all thought of the future. From the black vessel they saw a boat put

off, and they watched its approach as listlessly as if it were but the shadow of a
cloud on the water. The sound of the oars
was like the measured far-off beat of the
wings of a flying swan. The men landed
and seemed to murmur to one another in
the ancient language of the happy gods;
they lifted up the maidens, and their touch
was gentle as the caress of a child. Then
the day melted into the dark of evening,
and one and all the maidens sank into
quiet, dreamless slumber.

CHAPTER IV.

THE MIGHT OF SKILL.

WHEN Daphne awoke she found herself lying on a luxurious couch, in a low apartment lighted with hanging lamps. From the movement, she judged they were on the sea. Her companions were still sleeping, but the women slaves were awake, and moved about easily.

Daphne arose and tried to walk, but her feet were unsteady with the movement. She called a slave-girl, and with her help reached the door. She found, from the slave's report, they had slept a very long time—how long she knew not.

Outside the door was a kind of ladder. She climbed up into the fresh air, and found herself on the deck of a large ship. A vessel of some kind it certainly was, for no land was in sight — nothing but the waves dancing in the sunlight. But the craft was altogether different from anything she had heard of or imagined.

No sail was set, nor did there appear to be any masts. There were no oars, and no places where oars might be used. The floor on which she stood was a smooth unbroken surface, except for the entrance by which she had ascended, and two of a similar kind in different places, of which the doors were closed. No man was visible, and there was no sound except the lapping of the waves.

At first she thought some dreadful storm must have carried away the upper part of the vessel, and left only the lower portion; but on looking, she found no signs of break-

age or wreck, and discovered, to her amazement, that the sides of the bulwarks round
the deck were of iron, or some metal, perfectly finished.

The wind seemed very strong, but the
waves hardly moved. She saw some birds
in the water, which were, she thought,
swimming at a great pace without any
effort; then some beams passed with the
same speed; then, as she looked more carefully, the waves of the sea seemed rushing
past and breaking on the bows of the vessel. At last she found that it was the ship
which, without sail or oar, or any visible
power, was dashing through the water.
She was awe-struck! Alone in the midst
of the sea, with no sign of human power,
the vessel was rushing through the water
like some huge sea-monster!

She made her way to the side, almost
expecting to see great fins ploughing the

water, or a myriad arms clutching it in
swimming. But she could see nothing,
and hear nothing. Silently, without a jar
or shock of any kind, the vessel sped on its
way through a desolate waste of waters.
The silence and solitude terrified her, and
she turned to call her companions. She
wished to know if she were still in a land
of dreams, and under the power of the
drug.

But the sun shone with burning heat,
the spray of the water was cold, the air was
fresh, and everything she touched and saw
seemed real and true. No phantom sea or
ocean, she thought, could look so strong
and glaring.

Suddenly the Egyptian leader stood by
her side, and as she shrank from him, he
said, "Fear not! I have sworn an oath that
cannot be broken."

And when she looked in his eyes, her

courage was restored, and she said, "Tell me whither we are going, and how it is that the vessel moves without sail or oars. To me it seems like wicked magic."

"We are going," he replied, "to a country in which, if thou wilt, thou shalt be a great queen; and there is no magic, but simply human skill which moves the ship, though it would be tedious to explain the matter more fully."

Then Daphne mused for a time on the strangeness of her situation, and at length, after gazing fixedly at the Egyptian, she said, "Grant me one more promise." And he said, "If it is possible, I will grant it."

"Already when we were still at Athens," she said, "I noticed thou toldest the other maidens things that thou knewest to be false, taking advantage of their ignorance. Now I am altogether in thy power and at thy mercy, and I am prepared for my fate, having escaped a horrible death through thy aid. But my request is this : whatever thou sayest to me, let it be truth—do not play with me at least, with idle tales."

The Egyptian seemed to reflect for a long time, and his look became gloomy.

Then he said : "Already I have promised thee more than I intended, and the truth is too hard for thee to hear, or even to understand, for the present."

For a moment Daphne shuddered, but by an effort she recovered her composure, and said : "To avoid death by the pestilence, willingly, with my eyes open, I surrendered myself to thee, although I did not know even thy name. I look on myself as already in the under-world. Nothing now will terrify me, for thy vaunted oath I believe no longer."

The Egyptian replied, "The oath cannot be broken, and whatever I say to thee

shall be free from deceit. But there are
many things that I cannot tell thee : whatever I say shall be true, but neither can I
tell thee everything, nor could thy mind at
present bear it, any more than thy eyes
could look straight at the sun. My country is in many ways different from Athens.
My name is Thoth."

At first Daphne was displeased to be
treated like a child, but her curiosity was
excited, and she began to ask questions.
The answers, however, seemed for the most
part to cause still greater mystery.

Suddenly she heard a cry of alarm from
some of her companions. They too had
awaked, and had come to join Daphne.
Just as they came near, at the other end
of the vessel two of the merchants appeared, and began to eye the maidens with
the look of curious contempt which at
first had alarmed Daphne. She turned to

Thoth and said, " Why are these men so hateful in appearance ? They fill me with dread, and terrify my companions."

A look of displeasure crossed the face of the leader, and he said sternly, " This shall not be. I will compel them to honour whom I choose, and in a short time I will give thee an undoubted sign."

CHAPTER V.

THE MIGHT OF CHANCE.

THOTH disappeared, and on his return said to Daphne, " It is necessary to encourage thy companions, and to show them that they have nothing to fear. They seem to dread my people, but I will make every man give them an undoubted sign of respect."

Daphne informed her companions, and according to the request of Thoth, they stood in a line leaning on the side of the vessel. He then summoned his men, and they awaited his orders in an attitude of the most obsequious deference. Then

Thoth advanced to Daphne, and taking her hand, said—

"Permit me to show thee honour."

He bowed and lightly kissed her fingers. Then he turned to his companions, and choosing out the man whom he had struck in Athens, he said—

"Kneel down and kiss the foot of this maiden."

The man's face showed a strange conflict of emotions. Amazement struggled with obedience, and the strongest efforts at composure failed to suppress his loathing at the indignity put upon him. At length, however, he advanced and knelt down, and did as he was commanded. He rose immediately, with his face pale with displeasure.

Then Thoth turned to another, and pointing to one of the maidens, said, "Ask thou permission to kiss her hand."

Next to Daphne, she was the most beautiful of all the maidens, and the most courageous, and to kiss her hand was an honour worthy of the noblest. But, to the surprise of the maidens, this seemed to be a most difficult and disagreeable duty. The man obeyed his leader, but he asked for the favour as willingly as a coward might ask for death. The maiden laughed at the obvious dislike, and thinking it was due to the seeming dishonour, and being in her nature kind and generous, she said, "Nay, it is not so terrible. See, I will kiss thy hand first." But the man drew back with signs of abhorrence much more strongly marked, and the maiden was indignant.

The leader seemed for the moment surprised at the failure of his plan, and then his determination became stronger than ever. He commanded the men to kneel before the maidens, and to say in the most distinct and emphatic manner, "We will honour all these maidens as we honour thee, O Thoth." He then dismissed them, but instead of having been encouraged, the maidens were more alarmed than before.

Thoth took Daphne aside, and said to her—

"How comes it that thy courage is so much stronger than that of thy companions? We must make another attempt to gain their confidence."

He then gave an order to his men, and they brought up on deck a strange mechanical contrivance. In shape it was something like the body of a bird, and was composed principally of a kind of wicker-work made from some shining metal. The lower part was apparently solid. In a few words Thoth explained to Daphne that by means of this brazen bird, as he termed it, a man could be carried with the greatest swiftness through the air. He commanded one of the men to enter the machine, and, to the astonishment of the maidens, in a few moments the bird rose in the air. It sailed round and round the vessel like a sea-bird in search of food, and then at a sign from Thoth returned to the deck.

Then he said to Daphne, "This aërial boat will bear with safety two persons. Wilt thou venture to ascend with me? Perchance that will give confidence to thy companions."

Daphne at once assented, but the rest implored her not to leave them, and said especially that they were afraid to be left alone in the vessel with Thoth's hateful men.

The leader smiled with hardly veiled contempt, and said, "That is soon provided for. See, I have but to draw this bolt, and the men are imprisoned below."

At a word the men disappeared, and the bolt was drawn.

"Now," said he, "enter, and in a few moments we will return."

Daphne and Thoth then entered the car, and again it flew round and round the ship. The maidens lost their fear in admiration, and one said, "To what height can the bird fly?"

Thoth replied, "To such a height that thou couldst hardly see it. It will mount the air like a lark." And to Daphne he said, "Shall we make a trial?" and she at once assented.

Under Thoth's guidance the car rose straight upwards to a great height. Daphne looked down with wonder at the vessel beneath, so far off that the maidens through the distance could no longer be distinguished.

Then suddenly she cried out in alarm to her guide. The vessel had disappeared beneath the waves, and there was nothing to be seen but a few of the maidens struggling and shrieking in the water.

Daphne looked at Thoth. His face showed most unfeigned surprise and vexation. For the moment he seemed to lose his self-command, but it was only for the moment.

Apparently without an effort he became as calm and unimpassioned as before.

"Hasten!" cried Daphne; "descend to the rescue!"

"It is impossible," he said. "All will be drowned before we can reach them; and besides this, the car can sustain no more."

Daphne looked with horror at the composure of this man, and began to suspect treachery. "Didst thou expect this catastrophe?" she said, trembling.

"Nay," said he; "nothing was further from my thoughts. I can ill spare my men, and my scheme has broken down at the outset. It will be troublesome to re-place the maidens."

The coldness of his manner seemed to Daphne unnatural and inhuman. "At least," she said, "make an effort to save their lives."

"It is useless," he replied calmly; "but as thou wilt."

They descended, but long before they reached the spot, the sea had swallowed up every trace except a few remnants of floating wreckage.

"There is no time to lose," said Thoth. "We must go direct to my city. The strength of my bird will just suffice to reach it."

Daphne sank down helpless and dis-mayed.

Thoth applied to her lips a small phial, and she was powerless to resist. Again she tasted the strange flavour of the nepenthe, and again care and sorrow were dispelled from her mind. She heard Thoth say, as if to himself—

"It is not possible that they would have dared to disobey and become traitors. . . . Yet they hated the women. . . . But what flaw was possible. . . . Truly chance is great."

CHAPTER VI.

A STRANGE WELCOME.

WHEN Daphne awoke from her trance, she found herself lying on a couch in a luxurious apartment looking on to a beautiful garden. The scene was peaceful in the highest degree. The sun was high in the heavens, and the air was laden with sweet odours. Strange coloured birds flitted through the trees, and seemed quite fearless.

For some time Daphne lay drowsily looking at the garden, hardly conscious of the journey she had made. The past seemed a dream, and the present a dream

within a dream. At last her curiosity led
her to examine the details of her chamber,
and she rose up. Hardly had she done so,
when she heard in an ante-room at the
farther end a clamour of voices as soft and
thin as those of little children, and yet with
a strange resemblance to those of grown
people in the fulness and quickness of the
articulation.

Suddenly, through the opening of the
curtain which half concealed the aperture,
a troop of tiny little people rushed and ran
up to Daphne, kissed the ground before her,
and then stood still, as if waiting for her
commands. She then saw they were really
men and women of the true pigmy race.
They were finely shaped, and had pretty,
well-cut features, and without exception
the most pleasant of countenances. They
looked up to her just like dogs waiting for
some notice to be taken of them, with

glances full of suppressed friendliness. It
was very gratifying to her, after the strange
dangers through which she had passed, to
meet with such spontaneous affection from
the little people. At a venture she spoke
to them in Greek, and asked for food and
water, and one of them immediately gave
orders to the rest in the same old Greek
dialect which Thoth had used.

In a very short time a table was covered
with all kinds of delicacies. The pigmies,
Daphne observed, were very strong, and
with incredible agility they avoided any in-
conveniences due to their smallness of stature, leaping on one another's shoulders,
and climbing with the agility of monkeys.

As soon as Daphne had finished her repast, her little servants conducted her
through a series of apartments, all appointed in a very elegant manner, and they
showed her with pride everything which

seemed to them most beautiful and useful.
They watched with evident glee, and yet
in a perfectly deferential manner, for her
surprise when they revealed some new
wonder.

Her greatest desire, however, was to
know who the little men and women were,
and this wish was only gratified to a very
small extent. Their position seemed to
them so natural, that they did not understand the meaning of her questions. In
each answer everything seemed to depend
on Thoth. To say that Thoth had commanded such and such a thing, seemed to
them final. They could no more explain
why they obeyed and revered Thoth as an
altogether superior being, than they could
say why the sun gave light, or a stone fell
to the earth. One thing alone was quite
clear—they were absolutely under the sway
of Thoth, and yet the relationship was one

of thorough love and confidence. They
had evidently been told to treat Daphne in
the same manner, and they did so with
the greatest joyfulness. They were indeed models of affectionate servants, and
examples of perfect obedience.

The admiration of the pigmies for Daphne
was immensely increased when another of
their tribe entered, and in an obsequious
manner asked her if she would permit
Thoth to pay her a visit, or if she would
prefer to rest and recover her spirits. The
little people were evidently amazed that
she should be treated by Thoth with such
respect, but they were too well trained to
have any doubt as to its being right. It
was Thoth's message, and that was enough
for their simple, affectionate hearts.

Daphne was anxious to see her preserver.
The vague sense of fear which hitherto his
presence had always aroused was dissipated

by the atmosphere of kindly veneration in which the pigmies lived. Thoth, she thought, could not be very terrible when he was regarded with so much affection by these childlike men and women.

On the contrary, he must be a kind and gentle master, in spite of the example he had given her of his violence at their first meeting.

Accordingly, Daphne answered with alacrity that she would be glad to receive her host, and immediately after Thoth entered and saluted her with profound respect.

Yet in spite of herself, a shudder passed through the maiden. She looked through his eyes, but could not see his thoughts. She was not afraid of any treachery or violence. She believed his respect was real, and yet a nameless, causeless dread seized her for the moment. The little people, however, showed such undoubted pleasure at being in his company that Daphne's anxiety vanished, and she ascribed her fear simply to the strangeness of the situation.

Thoth lost no time in explaining the reason of his visit. He dismissed the little servants, and reminded Daphne, with all the calmness and dignity of an experienced ambassador, of the real object of her journey. He repeated again and again that no pressure of any kind would be put upon her, and that after she had become acquainted with the city and its people and governors, if she did not like to remain and to form a queenly alliance, she would be conveyed back to any place she chose. In the meantime she was at liberty to use the apartments and gardens as she pleased, and whenever she wished she could explore the city under his guidance.

"Tell me," she said, "is this the land of the pigmies, and art thou the king?"

"I am not the king; yet in truth I might call myself vice-regent, and say that I have all the power of the king. As for the people, presently, methinks, thou wilt wonder if this is the land of giants."

"Will the giants be as friendly as the pigmies? Perchance they will frighten me. Are they huge and dreadful like Polyphemus?"

"Nay," he replied; "though I said giants, they are indeed but full-grown men. Believe once for all that in all our land there is nothing magical or contrary to nature. Thou wilt find the giants as docile and amiable as the pigmies, but their duties are different. Come with me and see them; and it will be more pleasant for thee if thou wilt assume a disguise such as mine."

Thoth then put on a mask, and wrapped himself round in an ample garment. Daphne did the same; and but for being a little shorter in height, she seemed indistinguishable from her guide. Thus they sallied forth to view the city.

Thoth carried in his hand a golden staff richly ornamented with sparkling gems.

CHAPTER VII.

THE WONDERS OF THE CITY.

At the palace-gate was a lightly built carriage with two beautiful horses, for Thoth informed his companion he wished to show her the city itself before he made her further acquainted with the inhabitants. By a winding road shaded with trees he conducted her to the summit of a little hill, and bade her look round.

She saw at the first glance that the city was built in a curious rocky oasis in the midst of an illimitable desert. At her feet were buildings and gardens forming a large city. The buildings were widely

E

scattered, and the whole place was about twenty leagues in circumference. It was surrounded by lofty walls, and beyond the walls, as far as the eye could reach, there was nothing but a burning flat of barren sand.

The green spot on which the city stood, with the exception of the little hill, appeared to Daphne hollowed out like a cup; and it seemed as if the ocean of sand might at any time engulf it. There were no gates, and the country seemed completely isolated.

A sense of forlornness seized on Daphne, and in spite of her courage she wept as she thought of Athens.

Her guide at once divined her thoughts, and assured her that she had only to command him, and once more to be bold enough to mount with him into the air, and in a few hours she would find herself in Greece.

Thus he comforted her, and her heart warmed to him for his kindness.

They then drove through the city, and Daphne was amazed at the magnificence and beauty of the buildings and the luxuriance of the gardens. She saw very few people, and those were clearly of an inferior rank. They were of an ordinary stature and olive-tinted complexion.

They stood still and saluted the masks with the most profound respect; and Daphne observed that the jewelled staff carried by Thoth especially commanded their reverence.

All the buildings, roads, and gardens seemed in the most admirable state of preservation and good order. The city was evidently inhabited by people in the height of prosperity; and the thing which most surprised Daphne was the apparent sparseness of the population. Her curiosity was aroused, and she asked Thoth if this place had also been ravaged by the plague; but he replied that no city in the world was so healthy, and that never in the memory of man had it been visited by a pestilence.

The answer reminded Daphne of the speech of Thoth to the people of Athens, in which he told them that their indifference to the plague arose from familiarity.

The reminiscence of the untruth was vivid and unpleasant, and she said to Thoth: " Which word of thine am I to believe ? This agrees not with thy saying in Athens."

He simply replied, " That was before my promise; but in reality both statements are true. We have had particular cases of diseases like the plague, but never throughout the whole population. Our wise men are great physicians—in time thou shalt know all."

"But how many people are there?"

"The total number of men, women, and children does not exceed twenty thousand."

"And is this the only city in thy dominion?"

"Yes."

"How, then, canst thou boast of conquering the world?—and thou didst say so. Thine oath was soon forgotten."

"We have long since learned that safety and power are not in multitudes, but in wisdom and skill. Our archers, few as they are, are equal almost to Apollo. Thou hast seen that we can ride through the air, and thou shalt learn that we can perform other wonders unknown to the rest of the world. But it is best to begin with the simplest things. I will show thee our lowest class of workers."

They drove to a distant part of the city,
and as they passed along, the signs of life
became much more abundant. The dwellings, though still large, were smaller and
much closer together. The people also
were different in appearance, and the
farther they advanced the more they increased in stature.

At length Daphne understood that the
great mass of the people must be giants,
some of them being twice the stature of
ordinary men. Their faces, however, wore
an expression of pleased contentment, and
they were most obsequious in their salutations. They were lightly clad, and the
symmetry of their proportion, and the
massive strength of their limbs, were a
pleasure to the young Greek, accustomed
to revere the great statues of the Athenian
sculptors. · She thought to herself how
easily a small band of such warriors would

break to pieces any army; but Thoth said to her, "These are the most peaceful and quiet people in the whole world, and the most admirable workers when strength is needed. Which of your Greeks could contend with the weakest of these men?"

He then ordered one of the men to cast a huge piece of rock to a distance, which he did with the most surprising ease.

The women in this quarter were nearly as huge as the men, and, like them, admirably shaped, and, in spite of their great stature, very graceful in their movements. Daphne noticed, however, both here as through the rest of the city, that the women always retired to their dwellings on the appearance of the masks.

But apparently to please Daphne, Thoth ordered some of the giantesses to approach, and they did so with every sign of being honoured and gratified.

Daphne was delighted to discover that, with the giants as with the pigmies, the source of Thoth's power was not tyranny. Evidently he was regarded as a superior being, but as yet she could not imagine in what the superiority consisted. It seemed as if the whole city was ruled by perfect obedience, resting on perfect love.

When she returned to her apartments her little servants expressed the most lively satisfaction, and Thoth left her in their care, promising, if she wished, to show her more of the city and its people on the following day.

CHAPTER VIII.

THE DISHONOURED STATUE.

DAY after day, Thoth conducted Daphne through the city, showing to her all its wonders.

They were always masked, and were invariably treated with the same profound respect—no one even speaking to them, except in answer to some question of Thoth.

All the inhabitants seemed to be people of great skill; and many of the arts which they practised Daphne would have thought magical, but for the constant assurance of her guide that everything was due simply to the accumulated knowledge of ages.

She saw black charred wood changed into beautiful crystals, and transparent fluids transformed to solid images of exquisite design. Time itself seemed to be defeated at the hands of these cunning workmen, for, in a few moments, she saw a seedling grow into a plant with beautiful flowers, as strong and healthy as if it had taken a whole spring and summer.

Space was conquered in an equally mysterious manner. In a few moments they were carried under the ground, noiselessly and apparently without motion, from one end of the city to the other. The powers of nature also seemed enslaved: the heat of the sun was made to turn vapour into ice, the air was constrained to lift great weights, and light as brilliant as the sun was drawn from running water.

To her amazement, Daphne found that the solid earth had been honey-combed with workings, and forced to yield up abundance of all kinds of treasures.

Streams of molten fluids were drawn from the centre of the earth, and compelled to separate into parts and to congeal into solid metals; and noxious gases were unloosed to drive intricate arrangements of wheels and all kinds of tools.

Daphne began, unwillingly, to feel for Thoth something of the veneration in which he was held by all the people of the place. There seemed to be nothing which he did not understand perfectly, and she thought that it must be this superiority of knowledge which commanded such respect. Her interest in him was keenly aroused, for he seemed compounded of opposite elements.

When simply speaking, he seemed as

passionless as snow; but when he removed his mask, his expression revealed sometimes a keen conflict of emotion. Though he seemed in general bold, determined, and inflexible, sometimes his eyes revealed a doubtful hesitancy, and pride and confidence often seemed to give way to despair and self-pity.

Once she said to him, "Is there anything left for thee to discover?" and he replied, with all gravity, "The very beginnings of knowledge are hid from me : my knowledge is a drop in an ocean of ignorance. I have climbed a blind path which, perchance, will soon be lost in a wilderness." And then he relapsed into a melancholy silence.

Occasionally, in their wanderings and explorations, Daphne saw others disguised like themselves, and treated with similar deference by the people generally. Even these, however, showed to Thoth, on sight of his golden staff, the submission of inferiors.

Daphne had been encouraged to ask questions on anything which occurred to her, and one day she said to Thoth—

"Are there any superior to thee? Art thou really not the king?"

"There is one to whom I owe the utmost obedience, and there are many equal to me in authority if they choose to exercise their power."

"And what do they?"

He hesitated, and then, appearing to remember his promise to answer, said, "At present they spend their days and nights in sleep,—they rest to prepare for great deeds. I am vice-regent."

A strange people, thought Daphne, in which the king and his princes are sleepers, and yet some say that is like the blessed gods.

.   .   .   .

.   .   .   .

Months passed away, and Daphne began to think that Thoth must have changed his intentions regarding her.

She had seen none of the other chiefs, unless those in disguise were such, and the disguise was thorough and complete.

Sometimes, when half dreaming, she imagined that Thoth must be reserving her for himself; but in a moment the image of his passionless face, which never showed any emotion save that of troubled thought, put to flight the fancy. A marble statue seemed more capable of love than this superlatively wise vice-regent.

Never by one glance or touch, or word or gesture, had Thoth shown the smallest sign of love for her. He treated her always

with the same delicacy; he never laughed
at her ignorance; and in everything he
tried to consult her wishes. Yet Daphne
was at that time one of the most beautiful
women in the world, in the full pride of
youth and health, and endowed with a
mind capable of great thoughts, and a
spirit of courage to the performance of
great deeds; and Thoth was apparently in
the very prime of vigorous manhood. The
man was a mystery to her—a mystery surrounded by mysteries.

Yet why had he brought her and tried
to bring more of her companions thither,
with infinite trouble and risk?

And why had he made such a careful
selection?—for the maidens were the flower
of Greece.

When her reflections were turned in this
direction, other questions forced themselves
upon her which hitherto a certain deli-

cacy had prevented her from putting to
Thoth.

How was it that his companions had
shown such repugnance and contempt for
her compatriots and herself, whilst Thoth
treated her with such deference?

Over and over again she tried to detect
in his manner some trace of dislike, but
without success. Was Thoth of a different
race?

Then she wondered how the women of
the highest rank were treated, and why
the chiefs should have sought for strange
women for wives. Many women she had
seen in the city, but none who seemed of a
superior degree, unless indeed some of the
masks were women disguised like herself.
At length she determined to ask Thoth,
and the next time they met a mask she
inquired if there were other women in her
position.

He at once said " No."

" Do any of the women of thy tribe use this dress ? "

" No."

" Do ye of the highest rank always seek wives from beyond the seas ? "

" With one exception," he replied, " thou art the only stranger who has entered our walls since their foundation."

" Then are all your women dead—are none of queenly rank left ? "

" There are more of them than of us."

" Are they not beautiful ? "

For answer he led her into a building which seemed to be a kind of temple. He unlocked a massive gate, and conducted her into a well-lighted apartment. In the middle was placed the statue of a most beautiful woman.

" Such," he said, " are our women by

nature. Greece has rarely produced such wonders of form and grace."

From the statue Daphne turned to the walls, which seemed to be covered with statuary and paintings, and she started back terrified.

A horrible fascination made her stare at the works, and her eyes drank in the meaning of the artist in a moment.

All the highest skill of the painter and sculptor had apparently been exercised to pour contempt upon women.

On the beautiful statue in the middle of the apartment a number of stony figures looked down with sneering hatred. This grouping she might possibly have thought accidental, but the pictures left no doubt as to the design of the whole chamber. In every case beautiful women were being treated in a degraded manner, and men of the same race as Thoth were depicted as treating them with absolute loathing and disgust.

Then in Daphne's breast fear gave way to anger and offended pride, and she said to Thoth—

"How dost thou dare to show such things to me? Is this thy respect and honour? Dost thou not know that man is raised above the beasts only by the reverence paid to women? I loathe thy city, thy race, and thee! Of what avail is all the miserable skill and cunning of thy slaves? A swallow or locust can fly more easily, a spider is a better spinner, and the tiniest flower draws more varied beauty from the dull earth. I scorn thy boasted reason. Liar and hypocrite! how canst thou stay in my presence? Throw off thy mask and let me see thy cowardly features livid with fear and shame. Let me see before I die that in this abominable spot one blow in honour of women has struck home. Take off that mask— wilt thou make me mad? Down with the mask, I say, or my reason will not hold till I can find a way to death. Thou shalt not make me mad, and keep me for thy lust and cruelty in this horrid den. Hast thou no dagger—no deadly poison? Let me die! Monster, make thyself human for a moment, and being human, slay me. I will not be maddened and polluted."

Such and other wild words spoke Daphne, every moment becoming more and more infuriated, and, in truth, approaching the verge of madness. At last she rushed at Thoth and tore off his mask with a passionate cry.

His face struck her dumb with amazement. Instead of shame and fear, she saw wonder and triumph depicted on his fea-

tures. Yet his look was rather like that
of a spectator in a theatre who applauds
a good actor, than of a man in real life.
Certainly he showed neither contempt
nor lust nor cruelty. The flood of passion in Daphne's soul was swept away in
momentary wonder, and she fell senseless
to the ground.

CHAPTER IX.

THE WOMEN OF ROYAL RACE.

WHEN Daphne recovered consciousness she was surrounded by her little servants, all of whom manifested the most tender interest in her welfare. She was still in the same apartment, but every vestige of painting and sculpture had been removed, except the beautiful statue in the middle.

Just as she opened her eyes Thoth himself was placing on the statue's head a wreath of laurel, and a number of the pigmies were encircling the limbs and body with garlands of beautiful flowers.

Thoth had resumed his mask, but removed

it as soon as he observed she was aroused. His features were perfectly calm, and saying " All shall be explained to thy liking," he departed.

The little people drew Daphne in a low carriage back to the palace, and she soon slept, wearied with her passion and wonder.

The next morning Thoth did not appear in person, but sent her a picture, which was obviously intended to soothe her troubled mind. It represented in the most accurate manner the room of the statue, with the walls bare and the image garlanded, just as Daphne had left it. But the chief interest in the picture lay in the fact that Thoth himself was represented as gazing on the statue with the most profound reverence, and as if supplicating for pardon.

For many days he did not appear, and Daphne found herself constantly looking at the picture.

Thoth was certainly a skilled physician, and had administered the best medicine to her mind. In time her repugnance completely wore away, and she forgot a little the horror of her recent anxiety.

Later she reproached herself with injustice. She should have waited for some explanation. And then, as the time went by, she began to wish to see her protector again, and to wonder what he meant by saying to her, " All shall be explained to thy liking."

Still Thoth came not, nor sent any message, and at last Daphne sent to him one of the pigmies with this request, " All is well. Come to me. I would have the mystery explained."

In a short time Thoth appeared, and inquired with tender deference if she had recovered from her vexation and anxiety.

He spoke as calmly as if it were merely some bodily suffering she had endured, and in which he had no part. But Daphne said to him, " Fulfil thy promise—tell me why I was taken into that dreadful place, and with what intent those horrible designs were made."

He looked at her narrowly, as a physician at his patient, and said, " I know not if thou canst bear it; and yet everything hangs upon this mystery,—the object of our journey to Athens—the nature of our rule in this city — ay, and the future of the whole human race."

He spoke slowly and with the most distinct articulation, and the last words were uttered with all the solemnity of a priest interpreting the signs of a great national disaster. He seemed even to increase in stature, and Daphne was overcome with his impressive dignity.

"Tell me everything, I implore thee," she said.

"Come, then," he replied; "but arm thine heart with triple brass, for this time it is living women thou must see. Take care, however, to stay thy reproaches till thou hast heard all. Know always that it is my intention to pay honour to thee, and through thee to all women. But the women thou must see first of all will perchance again alarm thee. Art thou strong enough?"

Daphne shuddered, but she was determined to understand the affair, and she replied, "Lead the way."

.   .   .   .

.   .   .   .

Thoth conducted her to a part of the city to which they had never before been, and they stopped at a narrow gate in a lofty wall. Thoth unlocked the gate, and they entered a spacious garden, in the midst of which was placed a huge building.

Scarcely had they passed through the gate when Daphne heard cries of alarm, apparently from women, and saw some figures vanish through the trees in a hurried, fearful manner. For the first time since she had come to the city she noticed signs of distrust and fear. Here, at any rate, Thoth's rule seemed to rest not on love but on tyranny.

Such was Daphne's first impression, for the women, if women they were, were plainly terror-stricken.

They passed into the building, at the gate of which a huge giantess of hideous aspect presented Thoth with a scroll, which seemed to be a carefully kept record.

They entered a large hall, and again Daphne saw the same horrible designs as before.

Thoth said to her, "These, too, shall

be destroyed, but first we must look to the living."

At intervals along the hall Daphne observed curtains, and stopping before one of them, Thoth drew it aside and revealed a small cell.

Crouching at the back, like a terrified animal, lay a woman, scantily clad in a tattered garment made of coarse hair.

Her figure seemed robust and healthy, but was rendered hideous by glaring streaks of paint and devices of unclean animals branded on the skin. Still more horrible was her head. She was evidently young, but she had no ears, no eyebrows, no hair. Her mouth had been distended, and her teeth were sharpened to fine points. She grovelled on the ground, as if awaiting torture, and Daphne's heart stood still with horror and indignation.

Suddenly Thoth addressed the creature

in an unknown tongue, and after repeating
the same thing over and over again, apparently made the woman understand and believe what he said, for suddenly she gave a
sobbing laugh and crouched to kiss his feet.

"I have told her," said Thoth, "that she
need labour no more at her appointed tasks,
and will never again be punished. But the
thing which pleased her most, and which
she could not believe, was that without
her request she would never see any of
the masked rulers."

"What were her tasks?" Daphne asked.

"It would be difficult to explain," said
Thoth. "They were all most irksome,
most useless, most trifling, but they were
exacted with dreadful punishments. She
had to count grains of sand, to unravel
tangled knots, to learn by rote strings of
meaningless sounds, and to discover all
kinds of intricate puzzles."

To confirm his words, Thoth destroyed the various instruments of labour, scattered the sand, tore up the parchments, and stamped upon the fragments of the broken toys. The woman seemed stupefied with incredulous surprise, like a dazed child just recovered from a fit of terror.

They passed on, and Thoth drew the curtain of another cell. Here again the occupant was a woman, but she was exquisitely clothed, and both face and form were extremely beautiful. She shuddered when the masks entered, and hastily began to arrange in a harmonious manner various shades of coloured stuffs. She looked anxiously, too, at the walls of the cell, which were covered with pictures. To Daphne the pictures were perfectly unintelligible, and yet they seemed excellent both in colour and drawing. They were such pictures as might be painted by a great artist whose reason had been destroyed by some calamity.

"Her task," said Thoth, "is to live entirely for colour and form — in all other respects she is less intelligent than a butterfly."

Daphne looked into her eyes, and saw at once that she was quite distraught.

Again Thoth repeated the same gibberish, and at last seemed to make the woman understand in a blinking manner that her life would no longer be made a burden. To Daphne, however, it seemed that the message of release had come too late—like longed-for rain after the tree has perished with drought.

Suddenly a thought flashed through her mind, and without asking Thoth's permission, she threw off her disguise and addressed the artist. At once she uttered a low cry of pleasure, and ran to embrace

Daphne. Then she turned to Thoth and spoke to him in broken words. At Daphne's request Thoth acted as inter- preter, and told her the woman wished Daphne to remain as her companion. Daphne wept with pity, and Thoth led her away, the artist in vain trying to repress a cry of despair.

Thus they visited room after room, and through all the variety of occupations in which the miserable women were engaged, the same features were conspicuous. Their labour was, without exception, either most irksome, most useless, most trifling, or else degrading, and yet it evidently re- quired the highest degree of cunning and perseverance.

In appearance, many of the women had been made physically most repulsive,—some maimed, some blind, some almost shapeless with distortion ; and those whose bodies had escaped, had been deformed to a much worse extent in mind. Without exception they shuddered on the entry of the masks, and showed their terror in the most undisguised manner. Apparently Thoth tried to take away their fears, and to inform them that for the future they would live happily; but they listened with dull incredulity, and seemed quite hopeless.

In the whole of this vast building there was not a single creature who could have kindled a spark of love in the heart of the most impassioned of men.

Daphne was sickened by the spectacle, and oppressed with a heavy weight of sadness. She tried to escape, but her companion told her it was necessary for her to see more, and that he would show her the least revolting of the women. Daphne shrank from imagining what worse horrors the building might contain.

When they at last emerged the very sunlight seemed polluted, and the fresh air laden with pestilence.

As they made their way to the gate, Thoth spoke to the hideous giantess, and she showed the same surprise as her captives. To her Thoth spoke in a tongue which Daphne understood, and told her that she was to be replaced, and that until another guardian came, she was to leave the women unmolested. The ogress ventured to remonstrate, but at the first sentence Thoth sternly cried, "Darest thou question me?" and touched her hand with the end of his golden staff, whereupon the monster fell as one dead. As if to excuse himself, Thoth said—

"There is no further use for her: it is better thus."

Then said Daphne, "Is she dead?"

"Yes," he replied,—"dead beyond all

aid; and to all her kind will I do likewise."

They passed through the gate, and as before, every one they saw treated Thoth with the utmost respect and reverence. But Daphne was silent, weary, and despondent.

The horrors she had witnessed seemed to pervade every nook and cranny of the place. Helplessly she walked by the side of Thoth, and the salutations of her little servants when she entered her dwelling seemed to be as unreal and distant as if they came from the sky.

She felt for the first time her reason totter—she had not strength sufficient to wish to flee from the place, or to rush upon her death. At last she wept passionately, and sank into a troubled sleep.

CHAPTER X.

THE MYSTERY OF THE WOMEN RESOLVED.

FOR some days Daphne was utterly pros-
trated with the scenes which she had been
compelled to witness. The present was
joyless, the future hopeless. If she requested to be sent back to Greece, she
knew not if the whole land would not be
desolate; and, worse than all, she again dis-
trusted Thoth, and doubted if he would
keep his promise. She began to fear
that she was reserved for some dreadful
fate.

Thoth neither came to see her nor sent
any message, but, as before, left the seeds

of hope to spring up in quietness. And as the days passed by, slowly and gradually the youth and health of Daphne began to dissipate the gloomy memories, and wonder and love of life took the place of heaviness of spirit and fear of death.

To her own surprise she again formed the wish to see Thoth, and at times almost believed that he would in some wonderful manner convert the scenes which she had witnessed into an unreal dream. But the belief was momentary and evanescent, and she shuddered as she thought of the plight of the miserable women and their deplorable state. Alive they were certainly, and living a life worse than death. Hope rose again, however, when she thought of the apparent kindness of Thoth, and then she tried to imagine that he was to be the saviour of the women who had been cruelly ill-treated by others. Surely, she thought, he himself can never have been guilty of such crimes.

When her thoughts had become thus kindly disposed towards Thoth, he suddenly appeared, almost as if he had been able to read what was passing in her mind.

His face was as impassive and immobile as ever, and he made inquiries concerning Daphne's welfare as if nothing extraordinary had happened.

But she shuddered at his callousness, and indignantly cried, " Unless thou canst and wilt explain to me the mystery of these women, never look on me again."

" That," said he, " is my present purpose. Listen with care."

Daphne signified her assent, and Thoth continued—

" In order to resolve this mystery, I must first make thee understand how much this city is different from others in every respect—a fact, indeed, thou canst not have failed to observe. Tell me, apart from these women, what thinkest thou of our people?"

"They are truly a wonderful race, and surpass dreams in their knowledge of arts and sciences."

"And, apart from the women, what sayest thou of the government?"

"The people seem happy and contented, and they appear to live in the utmost obedience to their rulers through mere love and respect—except these women."

"That," replied Thoth, "is the plain truth. There is no city under the sun in which the people are so happy, contented, and so easily governed—except these women.

"And how," he continued, "dost thou imagine this wonderful state of affairs has arisen? But it is impossible to divine, and I will tell thee.

"Many hundred years ago the father of the rulers of our people, a man of a Grecian tribe, held a high office in Egypt. In knowledge he surpassed all men, and in knowledge lay his authority. He devised many just laws, and was honoured and revered both by the multitude and by the king and his rulers. Had he not been thwarted, he would have made the Egyptians the most powerful people of the world. But he was betrayed and deluded: some time I may tell thee the full history—suffice it to say that he was ruined and subjected to dishonour through the love of a beautiful woman.

"Mark this—for it is the key-stone of our policy. He contrived to seize the woman, and with a number of devoted followers he fled away and founded this city. Of the pure Greek race were only my ancestor and this woman, and about half a score of women and men. The rest were aliens, but all devoted to him, and prepared to pay him most implicit obedience, and his knowledge both of men and things was so great that he could exact any obedience.

"He determined to found a new state entirely according to reason. The government was to be entirely in the hands of the wisest man, and this wisest man was to be first-born of this new royal race. For Thoth the first, as he is called of us, forced the woman who deceived him to become the mother of his children. And he believed, through the secrets which he had wrested from nature, that, by the careful choice of a mother, he could combine for the future the right by birth with the right by power and wisdom.

"It is this careful choice according to types which has provided this city with dwarfs and giants, and with workers of all kinds, with aptitudes for peculiar forms of art or science. Thou hast seen for thyself the results of the wisdom of the first Thoth. But as regards the rulers, he was determined that he would, in the course of time, utterly stamp out the love of woman, and replace it with loathing and disgust. To this end he himself treated the woman who had changed his love into hatred with the utmost cruelty and contempt. At the same time, in order to render her offspring healthy and intelligent, he compelled her to labour both with mind and body, and to live so as to unfold her utmost powers. How meet she was to be the mother of a race of kings thou canst judge thyself, if thou hast not yet forgotten the statue which was her image. Her sons were taught from their infancy to loathe their mother, and to regard their sisters as necessary evils.

"It would only be painful and useless were

I to tell thee more in detail; suffice it to say that in the building of the women thou hast seen the natural result of this policy, acted upon for many hundred years. Our women of the race of rulers are simply intended to be mothers of particular kinds of men, and in the course of generations the men of this race have succeeded in acquiring for women a natural hatred and loathing.

"Now thou canst understand why it was my fellows—who were also of the rulers, though inferior to me—treated thee and thy companions with such contempt, and also thou canst to some extent explain the mystery of the women whom I showed to thee. Thou seest only the will of the first Thoth manifested through his descendants. Two principles he has planted in all his people—perfect obedience to his vice-regent, for we say that our king is not dead but asleep, and love of knowledge and of toil.

Thus in all and in us of the ruling race, our strongest passion is hatred and contempt for women."

As he ended his narration Daphne shuddered, for she thought she read in his eyes signs of lust depraved by malignant cruelty, and that he regarded her with all the loathing he had just described. Then she reflected on her helpless condition and on the misery she had witnessed, and swiftly determined to seek a refuge in death. Already with this notion in her mind she had provided herself with a dagger, and with a trembling hand she seized it. Then she raised her courage, and looking Thoth steadfastly in the face, she cried—

"I at least will never be degraded, and thus I escape from thy snare."

She raised the knife, and was about to plunge it into her heart when Thoth seized her arm, and said—

"Stay thy hand,—thou hast heard but half the story. Dost thou not wonder why, hating women as we do, and being most strict in keeping our race pure, we have notwithstanding sought to bring strange women from beyond the sea, and that we have paid them honour—I at least to thee, —thou dost not doubt that?"

But Daphne replied with undisguised doubtfulness, "Perchance it is but some horrible device to make the cruelty more exquisite."

. . . .

. . . .

"Nay," said he,—"listen. A generation back one of our vice-regents, who was my predecessor in government and also my father, thought he observed signs of decay in the race of rulers. He applied various tests, and all gave the same result. There was a falling off both in mental and bodily power. It seemed to him that in some manner the training and the selection of the women had been faulty, and being confident of the good results of the plan of Thoth the first, he ascribed the fault to a want of rigour. Accordingly he redoubled the labours and increased the tasks of the women, and, at the same time, treated them with still greater cruelty, for his object was to bring the mind of women absolutely under control. But desirous of confirming his view by reasoning from the opposite, he brought over from Greece a female child and caused her to be received with affection by the common people, and at the proper age made her one of his own wives. But the hatred of women was so strongly implanted in him that, though he treated her with forced respect and kindness, he could not show her any real love. Yet such is the nature of women, she loved him though she lived in constant fear and wretchedness. So much did her lord despise her, that he took no pains to conceal from her the secrets of our government. He allowed her to discover that she was only the subject of an experiment, and that if her child did not show at an early age signs of superiority, he would be destroyed. The mother's instinct was alarmed, and, by the aid of her old nurse, she contrived to exchange her son with another infant who had been destined to become vice-regent.

"Thus, in a manner contrary to our ancient laws, her son grew up to become vice-regent. So long as he was merely a child, the mother contrived to see him and to pour upon him her affection; but when at an early age he was removed from her sight, she fell sick, and, as is our custom, she was doomed to death.

"She perished, and later on I found out

the fraudulent exchange, and that I—for I was her son—had, as it were by accident, become vice-regent. But I also discovered very speedily by tests that we apply in these cases, that I was gifted with powers far above those of any of the royal race of whom a record had been preserved. I proved also by the application of new tests that the real decline in the royal race had been greater than my father had imagined, for he had not allowed sufficiently for the accumulation of knowledge.

" Perchance thou dost not understand the whole meaning of this history, but it matters not, for thou canst not fail to comprehend the conclusion."

At this point in the narrative he paused as if in doubt, as a man who believes he has solved a problem suddenly thinks of a possible error.

" It is strange," he continued, speaking

more to himself than to Daphne, "that I, the vice-regent of the haters of women, should to a woman disclose these secrets. Yet there can be no error."

Again he paused, and then with firmness and dignity proceeded—

"Therefore have I determined, knowing that I am greater in mind than any of my predecessors, to utterly reverse this policy, and to restore women to a position of equality with man, and henceforth to deal with the ruling as we have always dealt with the subject race. Yet, fearing the effects of long subservience and degradation, I thought it best to go back to the origin of our race, and to bring maidens from the best State in Greece to form our new queens, as was the case with mine own mother. In all other respects I have kept up our ancient rules; and, as I shall explain to thee hereafter, I propose to carry

out to the full the scheme of the first
Thoth for the conquest and government of
the whole world."

.　　.　　.　　.　　.　　.　　.　　.

Daphne had listened to his explanations
with wonder, and a great weight was lifted
from her heart. Her eyes bespoke grati-
tude and admiration. For a moment she
desired to throw herself into his arms, to
pour her soul into his, and, so quick is
thought, to love with all her being the
man whom but lately she had abhorred.

It was, however, for a moment only that
joyous thoughts thus filled her mind; for,
as she looked in his face, she saw no signs
of responsive affection. As before, Thoth
appeared perfectly impassive, and if he
showed any feeling, it was simply the satisfaction of a philosopher who has explained
in an intelligible manner a difficult problem. He had, indeed, spoken of the change

in the treatment of the women of the royal race in precisely the same way as he might have spoken of a new method of building the royal palaces. Again the spirit of Daphne was bowed down, and her hopes vanished. Thoth, it seemed to her, if no longer a monster, was yet not a man.

She sank down silently on her couch, and waited for further explanations as listlessly as a man struck by a heavy blow waits for a return of his senses.

But not long did she remain thus calm and spiritless, for Thoth had by no means as yet exhausted his powers of agitation.

CHAPTER XI.

THOTH FORSWEARS HIS OATH.

"Before, however, we conquer the earth," continued Thoth, in the same unimpassioned yet dignified manner, "it is necessary to establish the new order which I have set forth in our own city. It is needless to say that this will be a matter of some difficulty. Thou hast seen for thyself how repugnant are women to our ruling class, and that it is their nature now to treat them with cruelty and contempt. Still, with us the task is not hopeless, and, indeed, is quite possible. For, in the first place, obedience to the vice-regent is by far the most powerful motive of conduct, and also, in every respect our higher ranks are slaves, not of any passion, but of pure reason. Therefore I could say to my fellows of royal blood—such and such are the reasons, and such is my will; and the obedience must follow as surely as day follows the rising sun."

As he spoke thus, a will of adamant shone through his eyes; but a moment afterwards the troubled look of one who thinks he discovers an error in his proof appeared in his face, and he paused for some time in deep thought.

"But," he continued, "it is no light matter to upset altogether the growth of many hundred years, and to depart from the will of my great ancestor, who in all else showed the perfection of wisdom. The ways of error are as many as the paths of the sea, and I must take heed lest

I go astray. Therefore I have determined on two things as preliminary. The first is no concern of thine, and I need waste but few words upon it. Suffice it to say that I will take steps to see that this change is approved by the first Thoth and all the vice-regents, as well as by the present race."

Daphne looked at him with horror and amazement.

"Surely," she said, "thou canst not go down to the grave and consult with the dead?"

"That," he replied, "is, as I said, no concern of thine. But nothing must be done to shake the bonds of obedience, and nothing left undone to avoid the possibility of error. The fortune of the whole world and of the future generations of men depends upon this act."

Daphne looked at him steadfastly, half suspecting madness, but his dark eyes gleamed with intelligence and firmness of purpose.

"Therefore," he said, as if speaking to himself, "I will be advised by the first king and all the vice-regents. In this manner obedience and the rule of reason will even be strengthened. This is the first precaution.

"The second safeguard," he said, looking on Daphne as an archer looks at an arrow intended for a fateful purpose, "is of more interest to thee.

"At first I had intended at the same time to compel all the men of the royal race to take for themselves honoured consorts of pure Grecian blood, but chance or nature willed otherwise, and thy companions have all perished—chance or nature," he repeated, "not treachery — not disobedience,"—and again for a moment he seemed to doubt.

"Thy companions have perished, and perchance it is better so for my purpose. For, after much consideration, I have decided that the best plan is to make at first a single experiment. Accordingly I will explain to our chiefs my reasons and intentions, and will offer them an example in my own person.

" I will show them that it is possible to honour women without the madness of love, and that the children born of equals are superior. Everything shall be done with full deliberation, and an imposing ceremony shall be invented to show that [am not driven by the passion which our great ancestor dreaded."

He spoke rapidly, and Daphne listened to him without grasping his meaning at the moment. His words had entered her ears, but had not penetrated her heart.

But in an instant every word became a flaming dart and pierced her to the quick, when he said—

"Therefore, in two months from this day, with all imaginable pomp, I will make thee my queen."

Daphne sprang up in the greatest excitement, and quivering with rage and indignation.

"Thou stony image," she cried, "know that I have not yet learned—no, nor ever will learn—to obey thee, unnatural one, inhuman! I would rather wed the lowest slave in Athens than thee. Has thy hideous descent left in thee no trace of manly feeling, and no knowledge of the heart of a woman? I would rather see the whole world desolate than mingle my blood with thine!"

Thoth listened to her with undisguised

astonishment, and replied to her quite calmly—

"But what more couldst thou desire? Thou shalt be treated by every one, from myself downwards, with the most obsequious honour. Thou shalt be queen of the world, and the founder of the greatest race the earth has ever borne. Surely thou hast misunderstood my meaning. Say in what I have failed."

Daphne was somewhat soothed by the calmness of the reply, but her pride was still wounded. She resented the coldness of Thoth's reasoning, and she replied with passion—

"What more would I have? I would have one thing only, the first and the last —love—human love."

"And what," said Thoth, with an appearance of intellectual interest, "is love? What more than I have promised?"

The innocence of the answer of this wisest of men disarmed Daphne.

"Thy honour and respect could no more kindle a spark of love than all the power of the ocean could kindle a little fire. Read again, if thou hast the record, the story of thy ancestor, and know that I must be loved as blindly as he loved the woman who, thou sayest, afterwards betrayed him."

She glided up to Thoth and took his hand. It was cool and steady. She looked up in his face, but his features were unmoved and his eyes passionless.

"Shall I tell thee," she whispered, "how thou canst tell if thou really lovest with all thy heart? I have never loved, and yet I know."

By the strange contrariety of her nature, she suddenly longed to make this man, whom she had just addressed with scorn, her ardent lover. For the moment she forgot herself and her situation. Pride and dignity left her, and she only desired, with all her force, to subdue this man. She spoke to him as if she loved him, fearless of reproach, unmindful of opinion.

"Love me," she said, "and one look shall make me tremble — one caress stop my pulses. My heart shall be lost in thine, like a drop of water in a burning desert. Nothing but death shall separate us. Wilt thou not leave the weary pursuit of knowledge, to read without effort the open book of my soul? Look through mine eyes—is not the prize worth grasping? Am I not beautiful, and throbbing with the fulness of youthful life? See, my hand trembles in thine, and for one look of love I would kiss thy lips."

She spoke as if in a dream; but suddenly the hardness of Thoth, like the blow of cold steel, dispelled the fascination. She shrank back, her cheeks burned with shame, and she hid her face with her hands.

Then Thoth spoke to her words which tore her heart in pieces, and made her helpless with dismay.

"I regret," he said, "that thou hast utterly failed to grasp my purpose and to understand my position. Dost thou think that I will surrender my soul to the madness of love? Shall I keep at my side a passionate creature who will seek to betray and thwart me, and destroy by her animal nature the toil of generations? It is easy for me to imitate my father, and to bring a child from Greece to train according to my will.

"Surely I will do this; and as for thee, thou shalt find a chamber in our women's palace, and thou and thy children shall be the slaves of my will. Henceforth my oath is no more binding than if I had sworn it to a dog or a slave."

With these words he departed.

CHAPTER XII.

A WEARY INTERVAL.

AFTER Thoth had left her, Daphne fell into the most gloomy train of reflection that hitherto had oppressed her since she arrived in this strange city. Before, in her despair some gleams of hope had always appeared, but now there was nothing but black darkness. She had begun to trust Thoth implicitly; after the many trials of his good faith, her trust had grown into perfect confidence, and now it was shattered for ever. She had seen in the man's eyes a most terrible manifestation of passion, and she had no doubt that she would be treated even more dreadfully than the women she had seen in the abode of horror and lust. Worse than all, she despised herself for the way in which she had in reality led up to such a climax.

Regretful thoughts succeeded one another rapidly. Thoth was evidently a great ruler, who had been accustomed to the most slavish obedience. He was, or had been, desirous of effecting a revolution in the treatment of women, and he had for months treated her with deference and tenderness. Had she rejected his proposal as calmly as it was made, had she not attempted to get fire from snow, at any rate he would have kept to his word and restored her to Greece. She ought to have understood how the nature of the man must have been distorted by his descent through generations of women-haters, and to have wondered at the advances which he had made instead of expecting the impossible.

Never, she thought, could she have become his wife, but she might have been his devoted friend. She would have encouraged him in his projects of reform, —she could have liberated her fellow-women.

Now all was over. She felt covered with shame as she thought how she must have appeared to Thoth,—worse than a sensuous Persian — a mere animal. How he must have despised her when she actually suggested that he should surrender himself to her, as the first of his name to the woman who deceived him.

She despised herself, and for the moment her spirit was crushed. She longed for some sympathy.

She called on her little servants—there was no answer. She went to the door—it was fastened. She was confined in solitude. She wept bitterly.

. . . .

But after a time her courage and resolution revived, and she thought of the only means of escape now open—death by her own hand.

The sun was high in the heaven, and the garden of the palace was still open to her. She determined to drink again of the freshness of life before she died.

She walked along the beautiful paths, and watched with pleasure the birds and insects. Earth and air seemed full of life, and death seemed terrible. She recalled the wretched fate of the heroines of her native tragic poets. Before she had often wondered why they had not put a term to their sufferings by a moment's pain. She knew now.

It seemed to her a thing impossible in

nature—deliberately to take one's life, even
to avoid misery. She repented that she
had not already done the deed when passion
had given her courage. The point of the
dagger seemed very cold and hard,—life
seemed very sweet, and in the glaring sun
the gloom of death seemed most black and
dismal. At least, if permitted, she must
wait till night.

Then she thought on what might have
been her fate—on love unknown and hopes
shattered.

Again her courage and resolution vanished, and she trembled. She longed with
every fibre of her being for some creature
to speak with. She almost began to talk
to the birds and lizards.

Suddenly her heart stood still with joy—
she heard through the trees the twittering
song of one of the pigmies, and she rushed
in pursuit.

She soon reached the little being — a tiny girl, playing among flowers. Daphne raised her in her arms and kissed her passionately with tears and laughter, showering upon her loving words and caresses. The little maiden responded with unmixed pleasure, and said to her —

"Why does Daphne weep? What is her trouble? I will run and send a message to our lord. Thoth is very wise and good, — he can put an end to any trouble."

"Alas!" said Daphne, "it is Thoth who is the cause of my distress."

"Ah!" said the pigmy, laughing, "that is what we sometimes think; but it is never right — our lord is very wise and good."

"But," said Daphne, "your troubles, little one, must be as small as your bodies, and this is a very different case."

"Nay," rejoined the girl, still laughing; "we, too, think our troubles very great

and very new. But Thoth makes everything right. Now I will tell you what
happened to me to-day. I was sailing in
a little boat in the fountain, and I got to
the centre and landed, and my boat drifted
away, and I cannot swim. I cried until I
slept, and when I awoke I found my boat
at my feet, and I am sure that Thoth had
put it there."

The charming simplicity and the guile-
less confidence of the little maiden renewed
hope in Daphne's breast, and she kissed her
and said—

"Wilt thou try to take a message to
Thoth from me? But, alas! for my punishment the doors are fastened."

"They will release me," said the pigmy,
"when they hear my voice. I have done
no harm all to-day. I believe Thoth must
have left me in the garden to be thy
messenger."

"But," said Daphne, "thou wast asleep on the island."

"So much the easier to leave me," laughed the pigmy. "But tell me the message, and I will run."

Daphne put down the child, and sat down herself, burying her head in her hand, and tried to think of a message which might move Thoth. Shame and pride, not unmixed with dread, made the task difficult, and the pigmy began to grow restless.

"Shall I ask Thoth to come?—once before I took such a message for thee."

At last, urged by her affectionate counsellor, Daphne wrote on a tablet these words: "Daphne still believes in the promise which Thoth made on leaving Athens, and prays in all humility that she may be restored to some Grecian city. She is not equal to the high position in which Thoth would have placed her. She is only a woman with the common feelings of nature, and no superior being. But oaths are binding even on the gods."

She sent the pigmy before her to the palace, for she was too anxious to accompany her.

After a long interval, however, she followed, and found the apartment empty. The pigmy had been liberated, and a repast had been set in the usual place. Hope again arose in Daphne's breast, though she still feared, from the absence of her little servants, that all was not well. She was too sick at heart to eat or drink, and waited in anxious expectation. At last night fell, but there was no answer of any kind. She lay down on the couch and tried to sleep.

After some hours of the deepest silence,

she thought she heard a footfall near the head of the couch.

She started up, and beheld Thoth two or three paces distant.

CHAPTER XIII.

TRANSFORMATION.

Daphne's first thought was, that the hour of her destruction had come at last. She clung to her dagger, and in the presence of actual danger her courage was restored to the full.

Her face was pale, but her eyes flashed.

She looked at Thoth, expecting him to utter her doom, but he stood silently with his eyes fixed on the ground, apparently in deep thought.

How long they remained thus she could never tell,—whether moments or hours. Time was effaced, and she and this man were all that was left in the universe.

At last Daphne broke the silence.

"What is my fate? Wilt thou keep to thy first promise or thy last threat?"

Then Thoth raised his eyes and filled her heart with wonder. A thrill of fearful pleasure passed through her frame as she thought she saw in his regard no trace of hatred or cruelty, but the overpowering love of a strong nature.

She was not left long in suspense, for Thoth said to her, with a trembling voice—

"Daphne, I love thee as never yet man loved woman. Against my will, against my belief, in a moment, love has seized me — love as strong and irrevocable as death that, too, comes in a moment."

Then he advanced towards her, and seizing her hand, kissed it passionately.

He tried to embrace her, but she drew
back, afraid. The change in the man was
too sudden and unexpected. She knew
not what to think. Delight was mingled
with distrust, and she knew not which
would gain the victory. His kisses in-
flamed her heart, but the horror of the
past was too recent to be altogether forgotten.

She longed to be alone, and yet, at
the same time, she wished to ask Thoth
a multitude of questions. She wished to
know his whole nature, and as yet she
was afraid to give him her finger-tip.
Overpowered by the conflict of emotions,
she sank down on the couch, and listened
to Thoth as if in a dream.

Thoth respected her diffidence, and for a
time reason again seemed to take command
of his nature, and he spoke calmly even
of his new-born passion. The words of

love which she had spoken to him, and which, at first, had made no impression, had, he related, as soon as he left her, begun to recur to him as if she were still present.

He was quite frank. He told her that he had ordered her imprisonment, and had even tried to think of the details of her punishment; but in spite of his strongest efforts, whenever he thought of her he recalled her passionate appeal of love. At first he was astonished and bewildered— the whole affair seemed to him incredible and ridiculous. But the memory of her grasp made his hand burn, and her beautiful face chased away every thought. Then came her message, and he felt drawn by an irresistible force to see her. It seemed to him as if hitherto he had lived in a dream, and had only just awaked to the reality of life.

Again and again he described to her the revolution in his nature,—by endless comparisons sought to show her how sudden and complete it had been. His love was the sun banishing night, and hiding the stars from the cold contemplation of the astronomer. It was the sudden rebound of a tall young palm which had been bent to the earth with thongs. It was a storm of burning sand, effacing alike the road before and behind. It was the cleaving by an earthquake of the solid ground, swallowing up in a moment man's handiwork for ages. It was the tree which blossomed once in a thousand years, the first flight of a bird released from captivity, the first living prey of the young lion.

Then after he had exhausted language and imagination in portraying the degree and violence of his passion, the natural bent of his mind made him seek for an

explanation which would make the unreasonable reasonable, and the ludicrous full
of dignity and pathos. He proved to
Daphne that life is not truly in the indi-
vidual but in the race : his race was a
giant whose nature had been distorted
for a long period, and then suddenly had
asserted its strength. The loveless lives
of his predecessors had, by a necessary
reaction, made him capable of an infinite
depth of passion. Love, instead of being
stamped out and crushed, as the first
Thoth had supposed, had only been stored
up from generation to generation. It was
a transcendent passion, which did not obey
the ordinary laws of life and descent. It
was part of the very nature of life, and
could only be destroyed by death. Besides
this, his mother was by birth a child of the
instincts and passions common to the races
of mankind.

The search for reasons brought back Thoth, as far as was possible, to his former calmness of demeanour, and he began to talk of the future. He assumed all the time that the declaration of his passion was all that Daphne had required of him, and she had been too much overcome by surprise to interrupt the torrent of his eloquence.

When, however, he spoke in a definite manner of their union in a short time, she was driven to take up an attitude of defence. Much as Thoth had advanced in her esteem, she could not at once respond to his passion, and she was troubled by painful reminiscences. She said to him—

"Tell me one thing in all sincerity. Wilt thou still, if I wish it, send me back to Greece?"

His face became gloomy, but he answered at once—

" I swear it."

" Even if I do not love thee ? "

" Even so."

" And if I wish it, thou wilt never trouble me again ? "

" Never."

" And thou wilt tell me everything, and explain every mystery in this place ? "

" Everything ; but, Daphne, judge not hastily and harshly. For I will change every law and custom that is to thee displeasing. With thy love," he continued, in a vein of enthusiasm, " I shall be greater in every way than my great ancestor. He has impressed his will on this race for hundreds of years, and I will impress mine for thousands, and thy will shall be mine. Thou shalt be queen of the whole world, and the lives of the races of men shall be fashioned by thee. No goddess was ever fated to have such

might as my love shall give thee for a
dower."

Thoth seemed completely transformed,
and his whole being was tremulous with
passion. Daphne felt her power of resistance failing, as the strength of a mortal
fails before the desire of some deity.
Thoth became to her the perfect embodi-
ment of manhood and of love.

She rose from her seat, and drew nearer
to him.

She looked through his eyes, and the
depth of his devotion seemed unfathomable. She could doubt no longer.

She raised her face to his, and he covered
it with kisses.

Then he whispered to her, "Tell me
what more I must do or promise. Must
love such as ours await some ceremonial
for its fulfilment? This is to me the be-

ginning of life. Choose thou for us what form the marriage-rites shall take, for I, alas! know nothing."

At once the spell was broken, for Daphne remembered the horrible unions which the haters of women had hitherto made. She shrank from Thoth, and cried—

"Leave me! leave me! How can I forget that the women of thy race have been wooed with torture, and that thou thyself in all likelihood hast gone through rites of ingenious cruelty. I cannot believe in a future that rests on such a past."

But Thoth rejoined with passionate eagerness, and with every sign of truth, "Believe me, Daphne, I myself ordained none of these things."

"But," she said, "thou hast permitted these terrible customs to live, and thy fellow-rulers have been guilty."

"Canst thou not," he replied, "separate

the past from the future? I, at least, have not offended in this manner."

But Daphne made no response, and Thoth continued—

"Every one who has thus done shall be punished in any way thou mayest choose —if thou wilt, with death."

"Nay," she said, "I will be guilty of no man's death."

"Then," said Thoth, "I will change their natures, as mine has been changed. Wilt thou be mine if, in a full assembly of our ruling race, thou art chosen as the honoured queen of the new era?"

Daphne remained silent, and Thoth said abruptly—

"I must give thee time for reflection. I know that I shall never change. In seven days I will come for thy answer."

He saluted her with reverence, and departed.

CHAPTER XIV.

GREEK AND BARBARIAN.

Hour followed hour with unendurable slowness, until the appointed day arrived for Daphne to declare her decision. With sunrise Thoth requested permission for the interview; but Daphne replied that she would meet him at noon in the garden.

In the absence of other counsellors, she had determined to take advice from the full blaze of the sun, and to listen to the voice of nature in the whispering trees and the peaceful murmuring of the waters.

At length Thoth appeared at the time and place agreed upon. A glance at his face showed that his love had grown with the lapse of time, and Daphne felt a thrill of delight.

He saw the look of pleasure in her face, and with a cry rushed to embrace her; but by a gesture she stopped his advance, and said to him with forced calmness—

"Thou still lovest me as much as before?"

"Thou canst not doubt it," he replied; and she read the truth in the trembling of his voice and the passion of his face.

"Wilt thou consent to my conditions— the firm resolve of my vigils?"

"I consent before I hear them," he rejoined. "Do with me as thou wilt."

"They are hard," she said; "but after what I have witnessed I cannot take less. First of all, every mystery of thy race and of thy power must be disclosed."

"I consent," he said.

"All thy people, including the ruling race, must accept me as their queen."

"I will compel them," he murmured.

"When I am thoroughly satisfied on these points, thou must return with me to Greece."

"I will go with thee to the ends of the earth," he murmured.

"And if," she said, "when I return to my country, this city of thine shall appear, as is possible, too dreadful a place in which to dwell, I shall be free to remain?"

"Thou wilt never wish to do so," he said, with resolution.

"And if, when I hear again the familiar voices of my native land, and see the joyous faces of the people, thou shalt seem to me an alien, and unlovable, thou wilt leave me for ever?"

"But this cannot be," he rejoined.

"I know not," she said; "but if it should so chance, then thou wilt consent?"

"I consent even to this," he said; "but it can never be."

Tears stood in his eyes; and Daphne said quickly—

"But if, as my heart tells me is more probable, I yield to thy love, and thy will becomes my will, then thou wilt, first of all, wed me according to the custom of the Greeks?"

"That will I do most joyfully," he said. "I will prepare to return with thee as speedily as possible." And again he wished to embrace her.

"Nay," she said. "Thou shalt not touch my finger again until we return to Greece; and first of all, there is much that I must learn of thee and thy people."

"Ask, and I will answer," he said.

"But," she replied, "I know not what to ask. Teach me from the beginning. Thy city is planted in the midst of an impenetrable desert, and thy people seem few in number, and yet thou sayest thou wilt make me queen of the world. How can this be?"

"Power," he replied, "does not lie in numbers. We have weapons unknown to the rest of the world. The secret of our strength I will explain."

"Then," she continued, "I would fain know by what spell all thy fellows are kept in such perfect obedience. And strange words of thine run in mine ears,—of death and sleep, of a king above thee in power, and of vice-regents whom thou canst consult. Even in this glaring sun the air seems laden with foreboding. If thou wouldst gain my love and confidence, clear away all these mysteries; for they seem to me in many respects contrary to nature, and certain in the end to bring down the wrath of the immortal gods."

CHAPTER XV.

THE DOOM OF THE FIRST THOTH.

" THE immortal gods," said Thoth, " are but the vague memories of great men, distorted in passing from generation to generation."

Daphne shuddered. " Dost thou not fear to speak thus ? "

" I fear not," he said, " to speak the truth. But listen and judge for thyself if the first Thoth, who was born more than two thousand years ago, is not greater and more to be feared than any god recorded in Grecian fables. Thou seest yonder the roof of a large building

into which thou hast not yet entered.
In that structure sleeps the first Thoth,
surrounded by many generations of his
direct descendants. Consider this well,
for what I say I mean in all its fulness.
This king and his vice-regents are not
dead, but sleeping. Thou hast heard of
the custom of the Egyptians of embalm-
ing their dead. That is but a foolish
ceremony, the reason of which has long
been lost,—it is the husk of the kernel
of Thoth's reason. He discovered a perfect method of suspending life for an
indefinite period, and in the prime of
his life his son and vice-regent, in ac-
cordance therewith, laid him down to
sleep. He and his brethren also, at the
appointed age, were clothed with the appearance of death, and a new vice-regent
appointed. For one day in every generation our great father is roused from his

sleep, to invest his vice-regent with authority. I myself was so invested; I myself have spoken face to face with this most ancient one. Never on this earth was any solemnity practised by man so calculated to ensure reverence and obedience. From the middle of the throng of death-like sleepers this man rises up, and in a short time feels again the full tide of life in his veins. He listens to the progress made in the achievement of his plans, and the growth of the power of his race. He commands his latest descendants to obey the new vice-regent, and having for one day put in force his reason and will, he again surrenders himself to sleep."

Daphne was awe-struck by this narrative, but with an effort she said, "And do not the other sleepers also awake?"

"They," replied Thoth, "are destined to wake only when the task of our race

is on the eve of completion, to take part
in our final triumph, and that is no less
than the conquest of the whole earth."

"Tell me," she said, fascinated by a
weird foreboding of horror, "how this
can be?"

"The task imposed upon us by the
supreme will," he replied, "has been two-
fold. In the first place, we have had to
make perfect mechanical contrivances, by
which we can journey with incredible
speed through the air. That this has
been accomplished thou thyself hast been
a witness; and for each of the sleepers a
car has been prepared which surpasses in
speed the flight of birds and the rush of
the storm."

Daphne recalled in all its sublimity her
own aërial journey, and she could not
doubt the truth of Thoth's words.

Then he continued—"But a harder task

was ours, and that also has been at length completed. We have now at our disposal the means of destroying every living being on the face of the earth. The day is near at hand when these sleepers are to become the messengers of death. The earth shall be made desolate, and in time repeopled from this city. In a few hundred years all the world shall be inhabited by many races and classes of men, all perfect in their kind, and all governed by the highest reason."

Then Daphne cried out in horror—"Do ye intend to destroy all people living except those in this place?"

"That," said he, "was the design of the first Thoth, and had the means been ready fifty years ago, such would have been the case undoubtedly. But, as I have explained to thee, I have formed the opinion that in his endeavour to exterminate love in the ruling class, the first Thoth made an error. Accordingly, we must save some of the best women of thy race, and if thou wilt thou shalt have the selection. Now thou canst judge of the truth of my promises, and I will make one promise more. Know that I have penetrated deeper than my ancestor into the mysteries of life and death, and thou and I can live in all the fulness of life for hundreds of years. Thus thou shalt be as a goddess ruling over the earth. Tell me, Daphne, if the prospect does not surpass thy dreams?"

He spoke with all the enthusiasm of a man who is on the eve of accomplishing a most honourable deed.

But Daphne answered him, glowing with indignation and anger—

"Thy projects seem to me abominable, and unutterably loathsome."

"How so?" he asked, with unfeigned wonder.

"Thou speakest as if all mankind were noxious serpents and raging beasts. To me, a Grecian maiden, thou talkest calmly of destroying the whole Grecian race. Thou wouldst found a universal tyranny on universal slaughter, and so degraded is thy nature that thou dost not see anything horrible in such monstrous crime. I despise myself for ever having listened to thy love. Kill me, torture me, abuse me, I am in thy power, but never will I share in thy unholy schemes."

Then Thoth said to her—"Take heed; even my passion will not bear such a strain."

"I would thy passion were turned to hatred," she cried, "for thou canst not hate me as I hate thee!"

For a time it seemed as if anger and

scorn would altogether destroy his love; but Daphne quailed not, and in her wrath became even more beautiful and majestic.

The struggle in Thoth's mind did not endure long.

"True it is," he said, "that I cannot hate thee; my love is overpowering. But I cannot shatter to its foundations the edifice which my ancestors have raised. Rather would I make the whole world lifeless. I will give thee a day to reflect."

CHAPTER XVI.

THE REVOLT OF NATURE.

At Daphne's request Thoth departed, but as he left her he said with great emphasis—

"Remember that I have spoken the truth, and if thou wilt thou mayest become queen of the earth!"

His words excited her heart to a burning activity, and thought after thought rushed swiftly through her mind. At first she tried to persuade herself that he must have told her incredible fictions, but the more she thought the less she doubted. She had seen enough of Thoth's

L

power to believe to the full in the truth
of his narrative. She had seen him with
a touch of his staff strike dead the ogress,
and she had had abundant proofs of the
absolute obedience of his people.

For a time, however, she wondered how
a few hundred men could possibly destroy
all the nations of the earth. She thought
of Thoth and his dread compatriots flying
through the air, and discharging missiles
on the helpless people beneath; but even
with this advantage it seemed to her that
numbers must prevail.

She said to herself, "Even Apollo's
arm would grow weary of such endless
archery;" and then, suddenly, she remembered how the arrows of Apollo had
smitten the Greeks before Troy.

Plague and pestilence had been the shafts
hurled from his bow. She recalled Thoth's
allusion to Apollo, and a dreadful pre-

sentiment told her that it was in this manner that the nations of the earth were to be destroyed. In the same moment all the circumstances of Thoth's first appearance in Athens flashed through her mind: she remembered the grim indifference of the false merchants to the plague, and it was but a step to accuse them of bringing with them to Greece this unheard-of destruction. She knew it had been ascribed to poisoned wells, that the like had never been seen before, and she became convinced that Thoth was the originator of this fearful crime.

Then she wept as she thought that perhaps already the whole of the races of Greece had perished. This now became the most urgent object of her inquiry, and she tried to bring back every word, every tone, every gesture of Thoth when he had spoken of returning to Greece.

With all the appearance of truth he had promised to restore her, but at the same time he had said she would not wish to remain : he had spoken of allowing her to choose other Grecian maidens to share her fate ; but why had he not sent before another expedition after the first had been destroyed?

Certainly the man appeared to have an overpowering passion for her, and under its influence he had seemed to speak the truth ; but then she feared he might have coloured his narrative to please her in what seemed to him the best manner.

Was it likely that a being so inhuman in other respects should hesitate at breaking his word, as indeed before he had threatened to do? From the past and present she looked to the future, and she saw at once that there was no time to

lose, and that she must decide on a plan
of action. But what could one ignorant
woman do against the mysterious intelligence arrayed against her? Plan after
plan arose, only to be rejected, and she
soon became aware that her only hope
of defeating these enemies of mankind
lay in Thoth's love.

Even here, however, there seemed to be
an insuperable difficulty, for she knew now
that nothing could ever induce her to return his passion, and she feared that a
simulated affection would only hasten her
destruction. How could she hope to play
on a being gifted with such knowledge and
strength of purpose? She dreaded also in
her secret heart that by some magical fascination her mind would give way, and
that she might be led, in the weakness
of a moment, to sacrifice herself to him.
She felt still how near she had been to

a complete surrender of her whole will to his.

Would she have the strength to resist?

Before Thoth returned, she had worked out her scheme.

CHAPTER XVII.

GRECIAN GUILE.

ON Thoth's appearance Daphne advanced to meet him with all the appearance of friendliness, although filled with suppressed emotion.

"Thou art," she said, "the most skilled of all physicians, and thou knowest well that time is the best drug for the uneasy mind. Forgive my weakness. The Greeks of all people are the greatest lovers of their native cities, and I, a Grecian maiden, cannot see why they should be destroyed. But I will listen to reason. Why, if I love thee, should we not live here, and happily rule this city, regardless of the rest of the world? Why not leave thy dread ancestors to their sleep?"

She spoke to him with a soft enticing voice, and looked up to him as to a superior.

"Daphne," replied Thoth, "I have already yielded to thee the utmost that my nature will permit. It is useless to ask more. For two thousand years my race have toiled incessantly to create a new world. They await their reward. If I raise them from their sleep, they will never consent to forego their plans. If I raise them not—but I tell thee that is impossible. Rise they must, now all is ready, as surely as rises the sun."

Love yielded in his eyes to fixed determination, and Daphne's heart sank within her.

"The task I have already agreed to,"

he continued, " is wellnigh hopeless. They
will never admit women to an honourable
place, unless they are assured beyond doubt
that the choice lies between love and death.
I must prove that my love for thee, in
spite of generations of hatred towards
women by my fathers, is stronger than
ever love was, and also that their attempts
to crush it have crushed at the same time
life and reason. I will strain every fibre
to have thee recognised as queen — but
queen thou must be, first of all, of one city
alone in a desolate world. And, mark my
words, if ever this is to be accomplished,
thou must aid me with courage and with a
love equal to mine own. I must set thee
before these men—face to face—and thou
must say and do as I bid thee. If we
fail, there is no alternative but instant
death."

Daphne, still clinging to hope, replied—

"I know little of thy race, and my wisdom is dense ignorance compared to thy wisdom. But, tell me, canst thou not begin with the living—with them who have not yet entered on their long sleep? Why should not thy fellow-rulers, as at first was thy intention, seek for equal companions? There are many maidens in Greece less difficult to please than I. Persuade or compel thy followers to do as thou hast done, and then thou canst show thine ancestors how well the plan has succeeded —after thirty years—or twenty."

"I cannot," he replied, "make such a change of policy without the consent of my great ancestor and his successors."

"Then," she said, "even thy union with me must rest on their consent, and yet thou didst speak as if thou wouldst compel them to submit."

"But I said, by force of reason and

will. Know, once for all, that unless they approve of my conduct, I will not proceed."

"And what is to be my fate, supposing they do not consent? Thou wouldst not leave me to perish?"

"I will do my utmost to save thee, and I will perish with thee if I fail. But fear not—all shall be well."

Daphne reflected, and every way of escape from the power of the sleeping tyrants seemed closed. She had hoped at least to gain delay, and had even tried to believe that Thoth might, through his love for her, disregard altogether the past.

The future seemed more hopeless than ever, and she began to feel the courage of despair. If, she thought, this man were slain suddenly, would not the whole power of the tyrants be shattered!

She said to him, "But if thou wert to

perish with me, how would it fare with the
sleepers?"

"We have never," he said, "imagined
that we could avoid all the accidents of
nature. If I were to fail, there are others
to take my place. In my absence in
Greece another was appointed vice-regent,
and for every conceivable emergency pro-
vision has been made. It is useless to dis-
cuss the matter further, or to delay longer.
This very day thou must be prepared to
face the assembly."

"And if we fail, whither shall we flee?"
said Daphne.

"Nowhither," he replied.

"And, after all thy promises, wilt thou
leave me to the mercy of these haters of
women? If thy love for me is real, and
if thou art prepared to die with me, at
least redeem thy promise and take me back
to Greece, and there we can await our

doom. Thou dost not think," she said, anxiously, " that the plague has destroyed all the Greeks ? "

" No," he replied; " I have no doubt that by this time it is spent, and that many survive."

" Then," she said, " if we fail, flee with me. In any case thou wilt be an outcast from thy tribe. And I am very young, and life is very sweet. I would fain see my country and fellows again. And in some remote corner of the earth we might escape with a few companions from the general doom, by thy wisdom."

She looked at Thoth in a beseeching manner, and his heart became hot with love. He seemed lost in thought for a long time, and then said—

" If we fail, I shall be, as thou sayest, an outcast; and the little delay that thou prayest for may be granted.

" Listen to my plan.

" I have discovered recently a most curious and powerful substance. I can, by breaking a small vessel, fill the council-chamber with a vapour which shall at once send into a heavy sleep all present, unless they are prepared by an antidote. The drug is the most powerful of all our agents of destruction yet discovered. In a few hours the sleep will end in irrevocable death unless the remedy is applied, and then the recovery is slow. For love of thee, if we fail, I will use this means for a little delay. We will then prepare everything for flight, and only just before we depart will I administer the remedy.

" Thus we may gain a few hours' start, and in essence I shall not fail in my obedience. But I hope for a better result, and that reason will prevail, and thou wilt become the queen of the earth, and not a wanderer over a desolate earth with an outcast man. Rouse thy courage, and at the fitting time be prepared to speak as I shall bid thee. Let them see that thou art worthy of the highest honour."

" What must I say?"

" After," he replied, " I have explained the reasons for restoring women to love and honour, thou must say two things.

" First, thou must profess the most profound admiration for everything in this city, and, with all the excess usual in a pervert, encourage them to hasten the destruction of the earth."

" That is a hard task," she replied.

" Why?" he asked. " War is the greatest course of glory, and universal conquest might dazzle the most ambitious. All that we propose is war, on a scale and in a manner hitherto not attempted."

" Thy words," she said, " throw a new

light on the matter. Truly war and conquest are glorious, and the more thorough
the more glorious. Greeks have before
this warred on Greeks; and ye are, in
your origin, Greek. My former disgust
seems to me most unreasonable. Trust
me, I will aid thee to the best of my
power."

"Next," he said, "thou must express
thy ardent desire to leave the real government with the men, as before, and allow
that women are by nature inferior, and
that they may be loved and honoured to
the utmost without fear. Thou must say
that other Greek maidens would be more
submissive than thou."

"This also," she said, "seems to me
most reasonable. The arts and sciences
practised in this city seem to me wondrous
mysteries that no woman could ever pene-
trate. Women are born to admire power

in others, not to exercise it themselves. Consider how soon I have yielded my whole will to thine."

Thoth was rejoiced beyond measure with these words, and the wisest of men believed with all the simplicity of a child that Daphne spoke the truth.

But in her heart she had devised a cunning plan by which, unaided, she contemplated the greatest deed.

CHAPTER XVIII.

THE ASSEMBLY OF ANCESTORS.

AFTER some time Thoth returned and informed Daphne that all was ready. He clad her in her disguise, and told her to keep herself covered until he ordered otherwise.

They paused before the building in which the council-chamber was situated, and Thoth produced a small cake and divided it carefully. He ate a portion himself, and requested Daphne to eat also, saying it was the necessary antidote in case of need.

Then he said to her, "Be not afraid, for

first of all only those who are bound to obey me will have ears to hear."

They entered the building by steps descending into the earth, through a massive iron gate, which Thoth carefully closed after them. The clang of the iron sounded horribly, and the dim light made everything appear weird and sombre.

They passed through many devious passages, and every one, after they entered, was closed by a similar massive door.

At length they reached a spacious vault. In the centre was a kind of platform, and in the midst a curiously carved chair. Upon this chair sat a man with closed eyes and pallid face. To Daphne he seemed the image of Thoth.

She glanced round the immense chamber, and it seemed almost filled with similar stone chairs, and in each of them sat a pallid motionless figure. They were ar-

ranged in circles round the central throne,
but for a radius of a score of paces there
were none of the sleeping figures. In this
open space, however, immediately before the
central figure, stood about fifty men in the
same garments as Thoth, but not masked.

Thoth, accompanied by Daphne, advanced
to the front, and as they did so they were
saluted by a profound obeisance, in perfect
silence.

Thoth took up his position beside the
central throne, and placed Daphne on his
right hand.

"Are all the fitting preparations made?
Have all our ancestors been brought to
the light and set upon their thrones?"

A murmur of assent arose.

Then he spoke to the cloaked figures in a
low clear voice—

"At length the day of our triumph has
arrived, but in the very hour of victory a

most difficult problem has arisen. In every respect save one the wisdom of our revered ancestor"—and he turned to the sleeping figure—" has proved faultless. But the continuous degradation of the women of our race has failed in both its objects. For, in the first place, I have proved beyond doubt that our ruling race has degenerated. With the single exception of myself, we are all inferior to our predecessors, and in the last generation, which should take your place, there is not one worthy successor.

" And, furthermore, this treatment has failed to eradicate love, for," he continued, drawing away from Daphne her mask and disguise, " I, your vice-regent, love this maiden most passionately."

A look of dismay overspread the faces of his audience. They started back, as if some monster, and not a most beautiful woman, had been revealed to them. Amazed and confounded, they gazed on one another like men suddenly stricken with hopeless foolishness.

Thoth eyed them for a time with curious contempt, and then continued—

"Degenerate ye are in very deed, but it is not you whom I must consult. Recover your senses, and prepare to rouse the sleepers."

Thoth then gave certain directions, and his comrades dispersed. In a short time they returned to their former position, and Daphne observed a peculiar pungent odour, gradually increasing in intensity, pervade the air.

Thoth took her hand and whispered to her words of encouragement. She knew that the eventful moment had arrived. Like a bird fascinated by a snake, she kept her eyes on the pale face of the sleeping tyrant.

In a few moments his eyelids began to

tremble, and a faint flush appeared in his
cheeks. Then he seemed to begin to
breathe again. His lips parted, and slowly
his eyes opened.

Daphne glanced round the chamber, and
saw that all the sleepers had been similarly
affected.

In a low voice Thoth said to her—

"Fear not. They will regain speech and
reason long before they can move their
limbs."

She roused her courage, for though she
could not doubt that the mysterious beings
were living, their eyes looked dull and
vacant, and she hoped that nature had become her ally.

The silence was profound, and moments
seemed years in duration. Surely, she
thought, this is but a momentary awakening of the dead.

Suddenly, however, she saw the eyes of the ancient king gleam with intelligence, and she knew that both will and reason were awake.

Thoth took his place in front of the king, and when he saw that his long sleep was broken, he bowed to the ground, and stood still, as if awaiting his commands. Daphne remained at the side of the throne, still unseen by the monarch, though in full sight of all the others.

At last the lips of the awakened sleeper began to move, and Thoth presented him very gently with a curiously shaped cup. He sipped at first with difficulty, but after a time took a full draught.

Then his face became animated, and in a moment he looked like a man in the full vigour of life. Still, however, he did not move, though apparently he made an effort to rise. He gazed fixedly at Thoth, and then spoke. The voice and accent of ancestor and descendant were the same.

"Thou art my present vice-regent?"

"I am."

"I see," he said, "for the first time a multitude of my race aroused from sleep. Is, then, our task complete?"

"It is complete."

A smile of majestic triumph passed over the face of the mighty ruler.

"The cars are prepared?"

"They are perfect."

"And the arrows of death?"

"Nothing living can escape, such is their abundance and variety."

Again the king smiled with gratified vengeance.

Then he said, "A few days will suffice to regain the full strength of life in our limbs —already my mind is as vigorous as of old. At last, then, I become the ruler of the earth, and the races of men shall for evermore be such as my will has planned."

For a time he seemed lost in an ecstatic vision, as if the present had faded from his sight.

Then he said, "This moment is worth all the toil and waiting."

He raised his voice, which every moment became more vigorous, and, speaking to the assembly, said—

"Rejoice, my sons, with me."

He looked at the faces of Thoth's companions, and suddenly his face darkened.

"Why look ye so amazed, weaklings? Feeble and childish ye seem compared with your fathers." He turned to Thoth. "Thou seemest indeed my son. Surely it is not possible that my strict commands as to life and death have not been obeyed? Speak," he hissed—"are these the best of thy generation ?" for they trembled and looked foolish.

Then Thoth knew that the moment of trial had come, and he said with courage and simplicity, and speaking as if to an equal—

"These, oh king, are the best of thy race of my generation, and all are born of unions such as thou didst ordain. Know, also, that their children are still more weak and feeble, and that thy royal race appears to be threatened with destruction."

The monarch grew pale with anger, and said—

"My rules have not been followed. Some traitor has been a victim to the guile of woman."

Then Thoth replied, "Hear me, oh king, with attention, and know that in one thing thy policy has utterly failed. The rest of thy people have become, from age to age, more vigorous and skilful, because their women have been treated with affection and honour. But thy royal race has dwindled. I am the son of a stranger woman, though my father was deceived and knew it not. That miserable being trembling there is thy true successor, according to thy laws of descent. Know that the degradation of women has failed, and thou must choose between love and death. My counsel is, that ye who have returned to life take for wives the best maidens of the ancient cities of Greece, and make honour to women the foundation of our new world."

Then he took Daphne by the hand, and placing her before the king, said—

"This is the maiden whom I myself have chosen, and, in spite of generations of oppression, I love her as passionately as thou didst once love the mother of our race."

The monarch shook with anger and loathing, and in vain struggled to rise. "Traitor!" he cried, "darest thou thus to speak to me? Strike this woman dead on the instant."

But Thoth stood motionless, and said, "Thy whole power has grown out of wisdom—listen for a moment to reason."

"Dost thou speak of reason to me, son of an outcast? Ah, that my strength had returned, that I might kill thee with my own hand."

"Revered king," said Thoth, "I only ask for delay. Thou shalt examine the case thyself. Without thy consent I will do nothing. I have been faithful to all thy commands. The arrows of death and the aërial cars are at thy disposal. Had I been a traitor and a victim to the guile of love, thy sleep would have passed into death."

" Hold thy peace ! " cried the monarch. " In a short time I and my true sons will be as strong as thou, and then thy doom will be swift and terrible."

A hoarse murmur of approval arose from the parched throats of the motionless figures.

Then the king spoke to his latest descendants—

" Are ye all traitors, weaklings ? Seize them both, and tear them limb from limb. Ha! I feel my strength," and he half rose from his seat.

Urged by him, they began to advance, but Thoth eyed them with scorn, and, accustomed to obedience from their childhood, they paused.

The monarch hissed with rage, and cried, " Advance ! seize them ! "

Again Thoth said, " Revered king, listen to the voice of reason." He was answered by a louder cry than before, as the multitude of those who had slept rose at last from their seats, and painfully and slowly began to advance. The king himself in a moment seemed to recover, and tried to seize Thoth. But Thoth easily eluded his feeble grasp, and saying—

"Once more, wilt thou hear reason? for I, as well as thou, have will and wisdom. One step more, and I plunge all of you once more in sleep."

"Thou darest not—thou canst not," cried the king; and, inspirited by his example, all advanced against Thoth and Daphne.

"Thus," said Thoth, "I dare and thus I do!"—and he dashed to the ground a vessel that at once broke in a thousand fragments.

In an instant every one except Thoth and Daphne fell to the earth, speechless, senseless, motionless.

Thoth seized Daphne by the hand. "All is over. Come."

They passed again through the corridors, and the doors clanged behind them. At last they reached the open air and sunlight.

CHAPTER XIX.

THE VICTORY OF LOVE.

THEY passed in silence into the palace in which Daphne had lived since she came to the mysterious city.

The pigmies hailed their arrival with their usual satisfaction, but Thoth dismissed them for the first time sternly. They entered the garden, in which the means for their flight had been placed.

"We have no time to lose," he said. "Very soon I must return and restore my kinsmen. Before nightfall the great king will be in full command of the resources of the city."

" And then ? " Daphne asked.

" And then," he replied, " his vengeance
will begin."

" Dost thou not think he will be convinced as thou wert ? "

" I have made an irreparable error," said
Thoth. " My ancestor is swayed by all the
natural passions of man. He has slept
unaffected by time. His first thought will
be to give us over to the most cruel destruction. If thou still desirest to live a
little longer, we must flee at once."

" I regret," she said, " the failure of thy
plans."

He looked at her passionately, and said,
" Thou canst never now be queen of the
world, but a little love is sufficient recom-
pense for me."

" Dost thou love me so much ? " she said.

" Above everything," he replied.

Then she went close to him, and twined

her arms about him, and kissed his eyes and lips, and said—

"Dearest heart, thou art greater and more godlike than all thy dread ancestors. Why wilt thou sacrifice thyself and me to them? Why should they ever awake?"

Thoth started back from her, and said, "It cannot be. I cannot destroy at one blow the men I have worshipped—and the generations of my race, and their work of hundreds of years. Far easier is it for me to perish alone."

"Thou dost not love me," said Daphne, "or thou wouldst prove thyself greater than this ancient tyrant. He is unworthy of thee."

Thoth only replied, "I cannot do this thing."

"Then," said Daphne, "choose between me and them. Unless they perish, my love for thee shall be changed to hate and loathing.   Choose!"

He looked at her face, and felt his will quail before hers.

"What wouldst thou have?" he said. "I alone cannot carry out the scheme of destruction, and without it thou canst not become queen of the earth."

"I would rather," she replied, "tend sheep with thee on a lonely islet of Greece, than be the shadowy queen of a desolate world.   Choose between my living love and this impious deed, which I am certain can never be accomplished.   Thou hast failed already,—thou hast made serious errors; chance and nature have baffled thee in the most unexpected manner.   Awake! arise! and leave this city and all its horrors, as thou wouldst throw off a horrible dream. Come with me!   Treasures thou hast beyond estimation, and wisdom and courage.

Thou shalt become a leader of living Greeks, and in a few short years the last remnant of these dreadful scenes shall fade away."

Again she approached him and kissed him.

"See," she said, "I will not let thee go. The crime is not thine but mine."

He said, "Leave me,—it cannot be. I will break their trance, and then we will flee away, as before thou didst agree. Time presses. Thou seest this shadow slowly creeping along. Before it reaches the spot on which we stand it will be too late."

He pointed to the shadow of a huge column, covered with curious signs and symbols.

Daphne clung to him and whispered, "Let it be to them who hate me and thee the shadow of death!"

She looked into his eyes with eager pas-

sion, and saw signs of yielding. She redoubled her caresses, and whispered wild
words of love.

.   .   .   .

The shadow came nearer and nearer.

She covered his eyes with her hands, and
showered hot kisses on his face.

The shadow was close to them.

"This," she said, "is love such as the
world has never seen. Let me lose myself
in thee."

The shadow had passed, and then in her
anxiety Daphne became cold and still.

Thoth roused himself and looked. Then
he uttered a great cry—"Too late; all is
over!"

"Art thou certain?"

"Every one by this time is dead beyond
recall. Thus ends the greatest scheme ever
planned by man."

CHAPTER XX.

THE RETURN TO ATHENS.

ALTHOUGH Thoth assured Daphne in the most explicit manner that the whole assembly of the royal race must have perished, she insisted upon instant flight.

The danger had been so great and the culminating events so appalling, that she desired above everything to be hundreds of leagues from the scene.

Thoth became silent and gloomy, and most reluctantly agreed to obey her requests. Daphne attempted to soothe him, and to make his deed appear great and noble, but without effect.

" Surely thou dost not repent?" she said.

He replied as if he had not heard her question—

" Canst thou not remain with me a few months in this city until I arrange some kind of order? There are none left now but the people thou hast seen, as harmless as sheep, and, without a ruler, as helpless. My brothers were weaker than I, but every one played some necessary part. If I leave the city without a guiding mind, a disaster is possible. Why art thou in such haste to be gone? Thine enemies are irrevocably dead."

" I fear even the dead," she answered. " I cannot stay in this place."

" Not even with me—in the first glow of our love?"

" Restore me to Greece," she said, " and then, if thou wilt, return hither and put in order the affairs of thy giants and pigmies."

"And this," he said bitterly, "is thy love, when for thee I have sacrificed everything."

"Restore me to Greece," she said; "I can stay no longer in this dreadful place."

He yielded, and in silence conducted her to the car. Then he said to her with gentle, affectionate persuasion—

"Drink again of the nepenthe, and thou shalt awake in Athens."

She hesitated, as if with distrust, and he said with a tone of reproach—

"Nay, if I intended harm to thee, there are still a thousand ways in which I could show my power."

She drank as he bade her, and again felt the strange soothing effect of the drug.

.   .   .   .

She was awakened by the words of Thoth.

"Thou art at the rocks from which we departed, and the dawn is near at hand. Here is abundance of gold and jewels. Meet me at daybreak in the same place in ten days."

He kissed her hand and said—

"I return to my people to set the city in order."

And without further farewell he entered the car and disappeared.

.   .   .   .

Some peasants found Daphne and took her into the city.

The plague had vanished, and she found that many friends and companions had survived. When questioned as to her journey, she said simply that the vessel had been wrecked, and that she alone had been saved, and after much toil and suffering she had been restored to Athens by a man of Grecian birth, who wished to take her to wife. She showed the treasures in token of the truth of her words.

. . , ...

Every day, as the old familiar life was renewed, the recollection of Thoth and his city became more odious to her.

On all sides she saw vestiges of the plague, and she could not efface from her mind the thought that he and his companions had first implanted it in Greece. How could she love a man who had done such a deed?

She began to dread his return. She knew not what to do. She feared if she let him depart from her in anger that he might renew the work of destruction.

She feared to disclose the secret to the people and those in authority. She doubted if, against his will, they could overpower him,—and in her heart she wished him no harm—least of all, death by her devices.

She could not forget the fate from which he had rescued her, and the sacrifice which he had made.

The appointed day arrived, and still her mind was divided by doubt.

Before daybreak she was at the meeting-place—alone. The scene of her former departure rose before her, and she wondered if again she could trust herself with this man.

.   .   .   .

.   .   .   .

The first light of day appeared, and she saw no one. The light became stronger and larger, and she saw, as it were, a large bird in the distance, advancing rapidly towards her over the sea. She knew that Thoth would soon be beside her.

Nearer and nearer he came, and she pictured to herself his face aflame with eagerness and love.

Suddenly, about fifty paces from the shore, without warning, the car fell, like a wounded bird, into the sea. Daphne waited in breathless expectation, and in a few moments Thoth rose to the surface, and, swimming with great difficulty, made his way to the shore.

She ran down to meet him, and when he reached the land, she observed that he was pallid with suffering.

The water at the place was deep, and the rocks rough and cruel. She bent down and assisted him to land, and as he felt her touch, a look of pleasure crossed his suffering face.

" Art thou hurt ?" she said.

" My bodily hurt," he said, " is nothing, but I fear to tell thee the whole of my evil fortune. My city, with all its people and wealth and power, is buried in the sands of the desert—not a trace is left. There, in the depth of the sea, lies the last remnant of our skill. I stand before thee a nameless, powerless man. Yet if thou wilt only love me, I regret nothing," and he looked with longing into her eyes.

"Tell me but one thing," she said; "assure me that thou thyself didst not bring hither the pestilence that destroyed my race."

His face darkened, and he said—

"That is long since past, and I have become a different being."

She shrank back, and said—

"At least, say that it was thy companions—that thine own hands are guiltless."

"Surely thou didst know before that I alone did it," he said.

Horror seized her, and she cried—

"How can I forget? How can I dwell with thee or love thee?"

But he said with passionate entreaty—

"Now I am altogether different. Since I knew thee, it is as if I had been born again."

But she looked at him with dismay and undisguised terror.

"Alas! these are empty words, and the dreadful deed cannot be undone. How can a man be born again?"

Thoth looked at her, and for a moment seemed to wait for some sign of relenting, and then he said, hopelessly—

"Then there is but one course left."

He seized her hand passionately, and she tried to escape.

"Nay," he said, "fear no violence. I have always treated thee with honour and respect."

She left her hand quietly in his, and he raised it to his lips and kissed it.

"Farewell," he said; "but hereafter,

when thou thinkest of me, remember that
my last words were true, and that the
man who loved thee was not the man who
did this wrong."

Then he turned, and, without a word,
plunged into the sea.

In a moment bitter repentance seized on
Daphne's mind. Her memory was filled
with recollections of the kindness of the
man.

"Come back! come back!" she cried.
"I believe thee! I love thee!"

But there was no answer, save the lapping of the waves on the shore.

EPILOGUE.

I, Xenophilos, physician and philosopher, having wandered forth to meditate by the sea, found Daphne in a swoon. For many years she lived affected by what appeared to be a curious madness, but before her death she seemed to recover somewhat, and out of her narrative I have, with difficulty, pieced together this history.

I will only add that the body of a man, like one of the Egyptian merchants, was afterwards washed ashore. Near the spot, and many years after, some divers found the remains of a curious, unintelligible mechanical contrivance, partly destroyed by the sea.

O

APPENDIX

APPENDIX.

(*The last chapter of 'Thoth' as originally written in 1876. See Preface.*)

PHILETOS lay dreaming—dreaming that he was still hunting the lion. And it seemed to him that after slaying numbers of inferior animals, he lighted on one of an immense size, which, as soon as he came into view, fled to the mountains. He chased it through mighty forests, followed it across foaming torrents, and at last on a lofty barren table-land, he appeared to be fast approaching it. But the lion, roaring terribly, suddenly rushed away, and in the distance he could see it like an insect on the grass. Bravely and persistently he followed, however, and at last saw that the lion was standing on the edge of a precipice, or rather precipitous incline, at the base of which was a deep black lake; and it seemed to be in doubt whether to turn and try and rend its pursuer, or to yield to fear and rush blindly over the abyss. On Philetos rushed, with spear ready to his hand, and he was now within a few yards of the beast, when suddenly it sprang down the mountain-side, as if panic-struck. In its course it loosened immense rocks, which formed an avalanche, following close on its track. Philetos, with straining eyes and ears expecting the shock of the rocks falling on the water, stood at the edge of the abyss. At length the lion fell into the lake, and in a moment the terrific splash of the avalanche was heard. Then Philetos awoke, and springing up from his couch, stood up, with the noise still roaring in his ears. But on awakening he had entirely forgotten the lion, and he thought that he had surely heard the fall of immense rocks into water. He looked on the sunlight that streamed through his chamber windows, and tried to shake off his terror; for he thought that the Egyptian had broken faith, and that the end of humanity was near at hand. Breathlessly he waited to hear if a second noise would follow; for he knew that now, at least, he was fully awake, and that if he should again hear what he had heard, or dreamed he had heard, his fears would be realised. Nothing seemed to break the silence but the sighing of a gentle wind in the sombre trees, and the cries of animals in the distant forests; yet still he stood breathless, and scarcely able to stand with excitement. Never in his life before had he been thus moved: in a multitude of perils by land and sea, his cheek had not blanched; without fear he had fought alone with beasts in the midst of the forest, with only the moonlight to direct his blows; without fear he had found himself in the pathless desert deprived of food or water; and without fear he had attended to the wants of men struck with the plague. Never before had he feared for his life; but now he thought that all his fellows—men who, even at first sight, had loved him, and showered on him gifts and favours; whom he had loved as much in return; amongst whom he had no enemies, save the Egyptian priest; and by whom he had been worshipped almost as a god, save by him, —he thought that humanity was now to feel the revenge of that terrible intellect, and man, woman, and child in a few hours or days to lie writhing in mortal anguish, or withering under the breath of the plague. And this it was that filled him with terror. Not now did he seem like Apollo, clothed with immortal strength and beauty, but rather like Niobe, expecting her offspring to be struck down by the darts of the far-shooter.

Suddenly the noise which he had heard in his dreams was repeated; now there could be no doubt. He heard distinctly the masses of stone striking the waters, and the rush of the waters over them. He knew for a certainty that the barrier of the temple, which was to fall and give access to the light of the sun only on the day when mankind was doomed to be exterminated, had fallen. What his dream had pictured as the plunge of the lion, had been the fall of the outer barrier; and now he had heard the innermost wall—the dreadful veil, the fall of which was to reveal the most terrible spectacle ever enacted on this earth—fall irrevocably into the poisonous lake. In a moment, he thought, the awful ceremony will commence: even now the dead are raised and eagerly expecting the consummation of their hatred; the music is breathing out the solemn, gentle strains, that will soon swell into maddening peals, and rouse the fury of the haters of men from its slumber of ten thousand years. It is no longer a thought: he can hear the weird sounds, which welcome the dead to life, and form a fitting prelude to the awful catastrophe. What can he do? Even now, though the Egyptian should have his hand on the key of the gates of death, Philetos imagines that could he see him

face to face, he would forego his revenge, and
dare to disobey and dishonour his ancestors. He
is certain that this is the work of the priest, and
still believes the Egyptian to be his friend. There
is one chance still: if he can gain access to the
temple he will plead the cause of men, and perchance save them. He rushes from his chamber,
and nothing hinders his advance down the dreary
corridor that leads to the temple gate. Fleeter
than the deer he passes along; the roof re-echoes
the tread of his feet, and the hollow clang seems
like the shriek of despair; the fitful light of the
few flickering lamps is pallid and ghastly, and
seems to fall with the greatest intensity on the
bas-reliefs, which he knows represent the final
sufferings of man. The thick humid air seems
to fan him like a wind, so fleetly does he run.
In so brief a space has he accomplished the
entire length, that hardly could the priest have
turned to bar the gate of the temple, even if he
had been aware of the object of Philetos. But
so engrossed were both he and the Egyptian, that
they heard not the advancing steps, and he passed
the door, and was already advancing along the
central aisle, before he was perceived. On opening the massive gate, a spectacle so terrible met
his gaze, that nothing but the lofty purpose with

which he was animated could give him strength and courage to pass through the temple.

Only once before had he passed through the massive entrance, and then a single lamp, carried in the hand, had afforded him glimpses only of the architecture of the place, where the Egyptians, wrapt in their everlasting robes, were waiting for the time when it should be permitted them to link together again the broken chain of life, and end their existence with a moment of delirious joy—of joy so intense as to compensate for all their life-long toil, and a voluntary entombment of a thousand years. Even then, when a thousandth part was not revealed to him, what he had seen had caused him to tremble. The pillars by which the roof was supported seemed of adamantine strength; but this was relieved by no graceful capital, nor was the surface smooth and polished. On the contrary, deeply engraven on the stone were unintelligible signs, and exact images of the loathliest animals and most noxious plants.

There were sculptured groups in abundance; but hate and destruction in their most horrible garbs formed the only theme. Here was a serpent enveloping a deer in its scaly folds; the deer had been designed with the most graceful form, but the marble of which it was carved seemed shivering with horror. There, again, was a man of unshapely form, but evidently of immense strength, with a brow that denoted the highest intelligence, and features that expressed the intensest cruelty, strangling a being of the most perfect stature and beauty. There were pictures, too, and in one of these, at first glance, he had missed the prevailing emotion. A number of maidens were bathing, as careless, unconscious, and graceful as water-lilies hardly moved by the breeze; but when he looked again he saw beneath the water a monster that seemed half alligator, half serpent, and yet altogether human.

These glimpses had filled him with horror on his first visit, but now the light of an African sun fully revealed the minutest details. The pillars with their engraven loathliness, the paintings and sculptures almost innumerable, seemed as if they had been suddenly endowed with life by the heat and glare of the sun. But they formed only an appropriate setting to the rest of the picture.

The robes which had hitherto completely covered the bodies of the Egyptians, had now fallen to their feet, and they were standing in the garb of life. Not even a face-cloth obscured

their visages. They seemed as if they had just
been struck dead in the performance of some re-
ligious ceremony; but, in reality, the reverse had
taken place. A closer examination would have
shown that they were just aroused from their
sleep, for their eyes were open; and though they
moved neither hand nor foot, nor seemed to draw
breath, the look of the eyes seemed not altogether
as of the dead. There they stood in close array,
all in the same attitude, steadfastly gazing at the
upper part of the temple—seeming only to wait
for some signal to open their mouths and speak,
and rush tumultuously towards the day—where,
arrayed in gorgeous robes, stood the friend of
Philetos, bearing in his hand two keys—the keys [1]
of life and death; they seemed as if gazing on the
sky, in expectation of the signal of life, on which
they would open their mouth and speak, and rush
tumultuously forward. But as men looking to
the gods for aught receive what they desire, or
in some sort what they desire, at the hands of
men, so the entry of Philetos seemed to loosen
their frozen bodies as the expected signal from

[1] The mystery of these keys had been explained in an earlier
chapter. The plagues were supposed to be locked up like the
winds in the cave of Æolus, and by turning the key of death
they would be blown about the world, whilst by turning the
key of life they would be rendered harmless.

heaven. Yet they moved not, for the newly given life was snatched away by a dreadful apprehension. But as he passed through their midst, a thousand eyes darted on him looks of fear, hatred, and surprise. In a moment, too, voices faint and low, as voices in a deep cave hardly heard by the persons above, assailed him on all sides; fierce and vehement words reached him, but they seemed as large stones hurled from too great a distance, which gently roll up to the feet of him they were intended to crush. He heeded them not, even heard them not distinctly, but with rapid steps advanced to his friend.

The priest, who at first had seemed thunderstruck, and too much astonished to say or do aught, now poising his javelin, hurled it at Philetos with a fierce curse. But wrath or fear misdirected the aim, and the javelin struck the sculpture of the wrestlers, and broke off the hand of the ideal of intellect and cruelty. The Egyptian himself seemed a prey to the most violent agitation; at one time he looked to his ancestors, and at another to Philetos, seeming in doubt which to obey. Yet he drew not his sword, nor made any effort to kill his friend, as in similar circumstances he had done before. On his visage, usually, even in the most perilous and exciting circumstances, as cold and immovable as marble, was depicted a most terrible struggle of emotion. On the one hand, the friendship for which he had already sacrificed so much, and which year by year had been growing in intensity, urged him in one direction ; but on the other, the purpose of his life, and the lives of his ancestors—the tremendous weight that accrued to this purpose by the already accomplished resurrection, the vividness with which he saw his hereditary object before him, and in addition his sombre religion, which had never ceased to have the greatest sway over him—urged him to kill Philetos. At length, as men driven this way and that by doubts at last appeal to chance, and then become firm in one resolution by the upshot of a most trivial event, so the Egyptian, when he saw the priest raise his javelin, did not attempt to hinder him, but seemed to decide to act according to the javelin ;—if it struck Philetos ever so slightly, to slay him at once—and if it failed, to renounce his ancestors. Accordingly, when not only did it not strike Philetos, but ominously released the fair statue from the grasp of its destroyer, he grasped Philetos by the hand, but remained silent through emotion. But the priest, whom this act seemed to render furious, thinking

that the fate of the world and his revered masters
depended on him alone, drew his sword and rushed
at Philetos. But he, for the first time in his life
enraged with a fellow-man, avoiding the blow,
caught the priest and hurled him into the lake.
Still the Egyptian spoke not, nor raised a hand
against him. Then arose a faint cry, yet a cry
which seemed in its purpose naturally strong
enough to have shaken the temple to the ground,
from the multitude who filled the temple. Yet
they moved not, but with all their efforts could
only look their hatred, and mutter faintly. Then
followed a deep silence, for Philetos, after slaying
the priest, seemed struck with deep sorrow, for
never before had he slain a man. At length the
father of all these haters of men, in a tremulous
voice, thus spoke, and as he spoke, not one of his
descendants, nor Philetos, moved ever so slightly, but in the deepest silence all gave heed to
him :—

"Verily thou art born in my image, and I
should think thee my own son, but that a multi-
tudinous murmuring, which only hundreds of my
descendants could have uttered, has cursed thee,
as I curse thee now. Think not that I, who have
waited for my vengeance these thousands of years,
will now stoop to entreat thee, puny weakling, to

do what do thou must; for I command thee on the
instant to slay this man, and unlock the gates of
death. Thinkest thou because I am feeble and
but half aroused from this deathly sleep, that
therefore thou canst with impunity mock me thus?
Nay, rather, but that Will which has kept me
fixed in my resolve, and has made these hundreds
keep most strictly all my laws, that Will, though
now it be manifested by a feeble voice, cannot
fail to force thy sickly nature as it listeth. By
the wrongs I suffered from the foolish race of
men, who would none of my counsel, though to
every tribe I offered life and peace; by the blood
which flows in thy veins, by the mighty ties of
nature, by the oath I and these have sworn, I
charge thee to do my bidding; tarry an instant
and I curse thee with the fatal curse. Darest
thou look on me, and these thy forefathers, and
still let doubt divide thy mind? I charge thee,
pour out on the world the measure of my hate;
unlock these fatal gates, and, unworthy as thou
art, look no longer on us, but cast thyself head-
long, having fulfilled thine oath. My voice
already fails—slay—slay—slay!"

Thus ended the father of the haters of men,
and the Egyptian drawing his sword, struck
fiercely at Philetos; but less violent was the

stroke than that with which the grass, bent by a gentle wind, smites the earth. He muttered—

" I cannot; thrice before have I thus purposed, and thrice have I failed."

Then arose a shriek of horror from those dying men, and the father of them all, with a low, feeble, passionate voice, broke forth—

" By the stars of heaven, by the caves of the sea, by mighty nature, mother of all things, who once articulately promised me this power over one man, I consign thee to unfathomable misery for a thousand thousand years. On the instant thou shalt die, and thy spirit herd with the loathliest animals. In murky darkness and loathsome air, now sinking in mire, with reptiles for thy pillow, now in burning sands alive with fiery serpents, thou shalt pass a miserable after-life; more horrors than ever I could devise shall be thy portion. It is spoken! I curse thee with the fated curse!"

And from the lips of those dying men arose the cry of " We curse thee!"

They spoke no more, but with tottering steps advanced towards the two who were still in the flush of life. Then murmured the Egyptian—

" Philetos, thou seest what I have done for thee; and now I cannot have my reward in

P

simply clasping thy hand, for then thou must share my fate."

But Philetos, turning his back on the advancing hosts, clasped his friend by the hand, and in a ringing voice said—

"Shake off thy terror; look out on the plains beneath; seest thou not the sun smiling on the forests?—hearest thou not the cries of the wild animals? Let us away and hunt, and forget this horror; see, all nature smiles, and mocks at the curse."

But that other answered in a melancholy voice—

"Compared with mine, thy sight is dim, and thine ears are dull; but seest thou not that black cloud arising?—hearest thou not the gathering storm?"

But Philetos answered—"Truly there is a cloud, but we shall hunt the more pleasantly; and what is rain in its season?"

"Speak no more," answered his friend; "but if thou canst not read the meaning of the storm, look over the abyss and tell me what thou seest in the poisonous lake."

Philetos darted to the edge of the abyss and recoiled in horror.

"I see," he said, "a huge monster with gaping

jaws, rearing his snaky folds out from the mire; and its eyes are like the eyes of men that hate, and it hisses death and misery. Let us flee—let us flee!"

"Alas!" replied the Egyptian, "thou hast clasped my hand, and thou too must die, and suffer torment with me; say thou dost not hate me—say thou wilt not curse me when we two shall be deep in horror."

Philetos looked once more on the monster, which had now reared its slimy head above the precipice, and he read his doom in its vengeful eyes. But he quailed not, but pressing the hand of his friend, cried—

"Fear not thou! What if we must be in torment for a thousand thousand years, shall we not ever after receive homage from thousands of men whom we have saved from death?—will not the shades after these few years pay us homage?—and shall we not again and for ever hunt together and live life in life?"

Then murmured the Egyptian—"If I am ever with thee, even such misery were bliss; yet let us not die by this loathsome monster."

So saying, he clasped Philetos, and turned the key of the gate of life! Then with a shout of triumph they hurled themselves into the abyss, and were lost in the depth of the poisonous lake.

Then arose a mighty storm, and the day was changed to night, and the temple rocked to its foundations. The haters of men fell to the earth, and with deep curses gasped out their breath. And the storm increased, and the earth trembled, till, with a shriek of despair, all the structure was buried beneath the waters.

THE END.

PRINTED BY WILLIAM BLACKWOOD AND SONS.

www.ingramcontent.com/pod-product-compliance
Lightning Source LLC
Chambersburg PA
CBHW030312270326
41926CB00010B/1332